BEST
TEA SHOP WALKS
IN SOMERSET

Elizabeth Fowler

Copyright © Elizabeth Fowler, 1998

All Rights Reserved. No part of this publication may be reproduced, stored in a retrieval system, or transmitted in any form or by any means – electronic, mechanical, photocopying, recording, or otherwise – without prior written permission from the publisher.

Published by Sigma Leisure – an imprint of
Sigma Press, 1 South Oak Lane, Wilmslow, Cheshire SK9 6AR, England.

British Library Cataloguing in Publication Data
A CIP record for this book is available from the British Library.

ISBN: 1-85058-650-0

Typesetting and Design by: Sigma Press, Wilmslow, Cheshire.

Cover: Horner village *(Graham Beech)*

Maps and photographs: Elizabeth Fowler

Printed by: MFP Design and Print

Disclaimer: the information in this book is given in good faith and is believed to be correct at the time of publication. No responsibility is accepted by either the author or publisher for errors or omissions, or for any loss or injury howsoever caused. Only you can judge your own fitness, competence and experience.

Contents

Locations of Walks

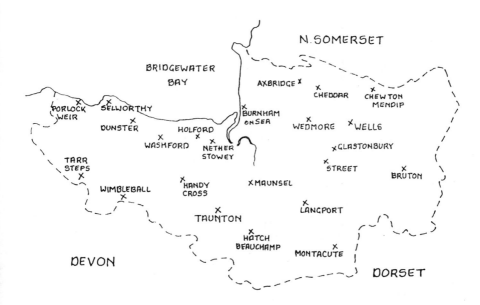

Introduction

Somerset is a county of wonderful contrasts. In years gone by, it bore striking similarities to Lincolnshire. Much of the land was either under water or waterlogged for most of the year. Being below sea level, it needed extensive drainage work in the Middle Ages to create what we see today. Indeed, even its name - *Seo Mere Seaton* is old English for 'people living by the sea lakes'.

Now known as the Somerset Levels, this area is rich in historical remains. There are extensive peat workings and miles of countryside with scarcely a town or village.

Contrast this to the hill areas, where upland areas surround the county, forming the borders. To the north, the magnificent Mendips bar the way. Cheddar, Wookey Hole and a dozen other fascinating points in this limestone range all offer interest and recreation to both visitor and resident. To the east, the downs of west Wiltshire offer similar isolation throughout many square miles without a public highway to be seen. The southern approaches are guarded by the Blackdown Hills whilst west, the brooding expanse of Exmoor dominates.

Then there are the towns and cities. One of England's finest must be Wells. It is certainly the smallest city and one that positively demands exploration over and above the walk given in this book. Taunton is another town of great historical significance, as are several that are not visited during the walks. The city of Bath is a magnet for visitors but it was removed from Somerset in the 1974 local government re-organisation, becoming part of the new county of Avon. *Plus ça change.* The last reshuffle saw the establishment of North Somerset, which is now the home for Bath. By the time you read these words; who knows where it will be.

But, despite the hills all around, this is not a book of hill walks. There is sufficient beauty and interesting areas in Somerset to fill many books. Thus, it is possible to select a range of walks, most of which are not too taxing, allowing the visitor access to all that is best without the need to kit out with survival gear, crampons and ice axes.

Motorists and holidaymakers chasing helter skelter for the perceived delights further west in Devon and Cornwall, often ignore this wonderful county. Do not join this rush of lemmings. Tarry awhile. Somerset is a gentle county to be enjoyed slowly. This is vintage Burgundy, not Beaujolais Nouveaux.

The alcoholic reference is deliberate and proves the point. Somerset is famed as a cider producing area. There are still orchards today, growing varieties of apples that the rest of the country has forgotten. Walk 18 visits one such manufactory. Those who have sampled the goods will acknowledge the soporific effect of this type of liquid.

Easy-going, laid back and a dozen similar adjectives all accurately describe this wonderful county that really should attract more visitors than it does. However, not everyone appreciates the charming features. Perhaps that is what makes Somerset so special.

1. Axbridge

Distance:	3 miles
Start:	Ye Olde Bakery Tea Room, Axbridge.
Grid reference:	ST 432546
Parking:	In the Square or a car park 200m away.

Until relatively recent times, Axbridge was something of a nightmare traffic-wise. Then came the bypass and a measure of calm has now been restored to this delightful village.

The Tea Shop

Ye Olde Bakery & Tea room is in the centre of Axbridge. Cream teas, hot and cold snacks and light meals are on offer. A variety of roast meats are available with jacket potato and salad. The sandwiches are first class and range from roast beef to cheese. Also, being a bakery,

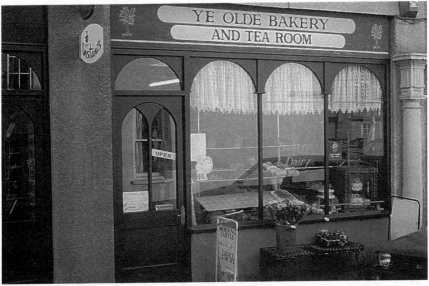

Ye Old Bakery tea room

there are freshly cooked pasties to complement the delightfully sweet and delicious pastries and cakes.

The Walk

Leave the car park, cross the road and climb the steps up to St John's church. Take the path to the left of the building and turn right to mount another flight of steps which lead up to the new road. Cross this road, taking care when doing so, as it carries very fast moving traffic.

At one time, this road carried traffic of a more pleasant kind. It was built on the course of an old railway that ran from Wells to join the main Bristol to the west line, near Yatton. Its name was the Cheddar Valley railway, but was also known as The Strawberry Line. This was because this glorious summer fruit flourished on the generally south-facing slopes. The produce was shipped out along the railway in the days before the lorry reigned omnipotent. Now, all that remains are the old station buildings.

Now there is a steep climb that lasts for some 600m. Cross the fence which was built at the same time as the road with the express intention of keeping livestock from under the wheels of vehicles. Keep walking straight up the hill, over the stile and ignoring paths that offer a route to either left or right. Then the climb eases dramatically as the plateau of Fry's Hill is reached. There is a radio mast to the right and, at 223m above sea level, the views on a clear day are outstanding. Well worth the physical effort expended in getting to the top.

The area of land to the left is known as Shoot Shelve Hill. Carboniferous limestone grassland is a rare and beautiful habitat and thanks to commoners grazing animals, this area has kept a good proportion of its open landscape and fine grassland. So rich in flowers and associated wildlife, that there was enough for English nature to include it in the Crook's Peak SSSI (Site of Special Scientific Interest) in 1986. Dropwort, birds foot trefoil and wild thyme are just some of the plants to be found here. As for the fauna, small tortoiseshell butterflies, buzzards and meadow pipits occupy the hill. Medieval rabbit warrens are still in use, whilst man's contribution is a disused tramway that served an ochre mine.

The ancient grazing rights that exist here are for 1570 sheep or equiva-

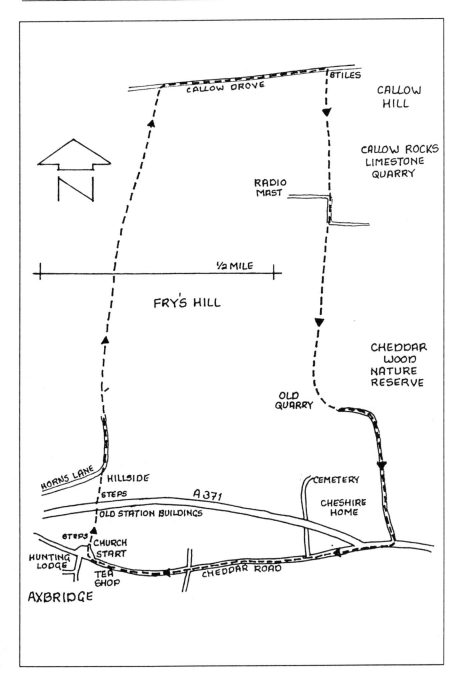

lent livestock and are currently held by 36 commoners. Grazing by these animals is essential to maintain and retain the open beautiful landscape. Shoot Shelve Hill is owned and managed by the National Trust.

The path continues north across a couple of fields until it reaches an east/west track known as Callow Drove, an ancient trackway. Today, this is used as part of the West Mendip Way. Turn right here and walk between the weather-beaten stone walls along the crest of this hill for some 300m. This track was used to form the northern boundary of Somerset at the 1974 local government reorganisation.

There are then a couple of stiles to cross before the walk makes a right turn just beyond the second one. This passes the edge of a limestone quarry on the left and becomes a very steep drop. There is a fork in the path halfway down; keep left. To the left is the extensive Cheddar Wood, which is a nature reserve. Keep left again at the next split which takes the walk past the back of the impressive Cheshire Homes building of St Michael's. On meeting the main road again, cross and turn right. After 100m, the new road roars away to the right whilst Cheddar Road bears off to the left and returns the walk to the starting point, passing the tea room on the left in St Mary's Street.

The village itself is worth a short stroll. Most impressive by far is King John's Hunting Lodge. This is an early Tudor merchant's house that was rescued and comprehensively restored in 1971. It is now under the care of the National Trust and open to visitors from Easter to the end of September. It also houses a local history museum run by Sedgemoor District Council with the assistance and co-operation of the Somerset County Museums Service and Axbridge Archaeological and Local History Society.

2. Cheddar

Distance: 4½ miles.
Start: Hillside Cottage, Cheddar Gorge.
Grid reference: ST 468540
Parking: Can be tricky. There are parks in the village and some at the lower end of the Gorge.

Caution: at several points, this walk goes close to a sheer drop over the edge of the cliffs. Take great care.

If there is one place in the Mendips that attracts the visitor, it is Cheddar. In season, the place is over-run. Normally, this kind of tourist honey trap would be avoided, but the attractions here are so many, the walking dramatic and the sights so incomparable, that the sin of omission cannot be justified.

Cheddar Gorge is probably England's best-known limestone feature. Some two miles long and up to 137m (450ft) deep, it has a road

Lots of shops and refreshment points in Cheddar Gorge

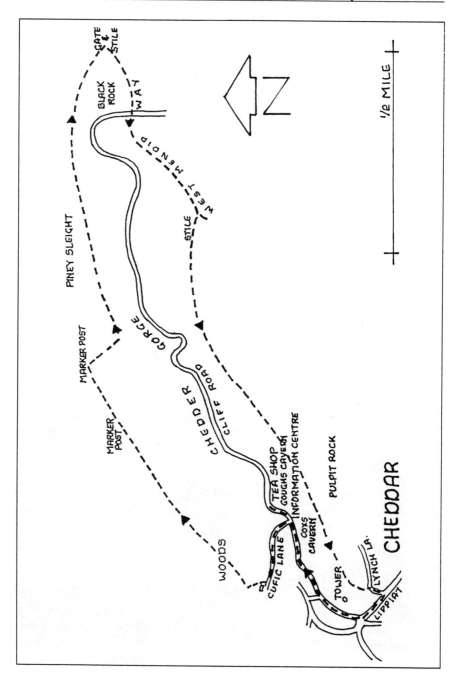

that weaves up through it. After you have walked around the edge, a fine way to see it from below is aboard the bus (usually open-topped) that runs from the edge of town through to the top.

The gorge was formed as a result of the Ice Age when the huge quantities of water released from thawing glaciers had to run somewhere. There have been several periods when ice has covered England, the most recent started around one million years ago and lasted to about ten thousand years ago.

One thing to note is that you will not be the first to discover this area. Evidence exists that man followed the retreating icecap following the discovery in 1901, of the remains of a prehistoric man in Gough's Cave. These remains are preserved locally. Later, the Romans followed. Remains of their tenure were discovered at Long Hole in the Gorge where a hoard of silver coins from the first to the fourth century was uncovered. In turn, it was a Saxon stronghold, then Domesday lists four manors here.

Today, the caves themselves are a huge draw, and rightly so. There are four hundred caverns and potholes in the area. Many are available to visitors and offer displays of superb stalactites and stalagmites. Many confuse the names between the formations which grow down from the roof and those which grow up from the floor. A mnemonic that at least the gentlemen will remember easily is, tights (or tites in this case) are made to come down!

Gough's is one of the most spectacular caves, stretching over 400m with the most elegant pillared chambers. Cox's is another well worth a visit. Here, an underground pool offers the most exquisite reflections of the multi-hued limestone.

The Tea Shops

Being such an enormous tourist attraction, there are cafés, restaurants and tea rooms almost beyond count. Most of the better ones are to be found in the Gorge. At the bottom, **Derek's Tea-Room** is good, as is the **Edelweiss**. Between the caves is the location of our selected establishment – if only because it is open during the winter.

Hillside Cottage is on the left-hand side of the steep climb that is 'The Cliffs', beyond the Cliff Hotel. Another ancient building, this one is over two hundred years old and, being set back towards the foot of Lion Rock, over the stream, it tends to be a little more peaceful than the rest in this area. Both food and drink are excellent here, the tea being particularly tasty. The cream teas are wonderful, as are the home-made cakes and pastry.

The Walk

Leave the tea room and cross the stream, back to the road and turn right. Walk down to the tourist information office and turn right into Cufic Lane. Follow this uphill and take the right turn by a cottage. The whole of this area is well walked. The various tracks are quite clear to follow as well as being well signed.

Take the next sharp right and continue up the hill. The path continues through woodland to a stile. Cross this and continue along the path, which has now left the trees behind. A marker post indicates that Piney Sleight is the next destination. Follow these posts, turning right and then left after 100m.

Already the views are starting to develop. To this end, there is a short diversion to the right which allows a view of Black Rock, where the walk will shortly reach. The nature reserve hereabouts is owned by the National Trust and managed by The Somerset Wildlife Trust.

Shortly, the walk will start to descend, putting a different set of stresses on your leg muscles. Cross two stiles, still following the clear track which leads back into woodland and the nature reserve.

In Saxon times, this area was a royal forest where the kings of England used to hunt. There is a story of King Edmund in 941 narrowly escaping death as first the stag, then the pursuing hounds ran over the sheer edge. The king's horse just avoided a similar fate. In thanksgiving for being spared, he elevated a monk, Dunstan, to Abbot of Glastonbury. What happened to the then incumbent is not recorded.

At the gate and stile, turn right. Here, we encounter the West Mendip Way again, previously used during Walk 1. This leads down to the Gorge Road. Cross and climb the hill and at the top, beyond a gate, the path splits. Take the right-hand one, waving farewell to the West Mendip Way which goes left, and cross two stiles. The walk is now steeply downhill and, at times, close to the cliff edge. Take the path to the left at the tower and through more woodland, down to a T-junction. A right turn along here delivers the walk into the centre of the village. Turn right again and walk back up to the tea room.

3. Chewton Mendip

Distance:	4½ miles.
Start:	Chewton Cheese Dairy, Chewton Mendip, N. Bath. Tel: 01761 241666
Grid reference:	ST 592526
Parking:	At the dairy.

There are several places in Somerset that make cheese and most of them have found that opening their doors to visitors is a convenient source of income. Not only do they create an interest in their product, but an almost captive audience are pretty sure to take some of it away. This adds up to good business: charge retail prices but cut out the mark-up added by both wholesaler and retailer. It's not all one way traffic though. The simple punter (you and me) get to try cheeses that the taste police (the supermarkets) generally forbid. One such place is at Chewton Mendip and, as they also have a delightful restaurant which serves simply superb teas, we will start a walk from there.

The Tea Shop

The selected establishment is upstairs. The old building has been greatly modified over the years, partly due to the increasing visitor numbers. It's a long, light airy room with polished wooden tables and floors where you can have your tea whilst watching cheese being made. On the menu, you will find superb home-made cakes, English wine, lunches and anything from morning coffee to afternoon teas, cream teas or a full meal.

From the upstairs vantage point, you can look through the large gallery windows down to the cheese-making areas below. Things start quite early, before the restaurant opens, but there are varying stages as the day progresses. If you arrive outside restaurant hours, or are not yet ready to avail yourself of their delights, there is an observation platform. Then, visit the shop and buy some of their really flavoursome products.

Tea room at Chewton Cheese Dairy

Many years ago, when both the world and I were much younger, I remember visiting this factory to buy a full truckle. This was taken on its seventy-mile journey home and divided between three sisters and myself. We each had large families, so the journey was well worth it. Twenty years on, the memory still surfaces and creates a giggle in family circles. They see me pulling up outside a family gathering in my open topped Morgan, a huge cheese sitting in the passenger seat, with its seat belt on.

To those who look aghast at a 140-mile round trip to buy cheese, I can only ask you to defer judgement until you have tasted the cheeses. If there is a heaven, this must be what the angels eat at tea break time. They come in a variety of consistencies; solid to crumbly and in flavour from mild to extra mature. Beware of the latter if your palate is adjusted to supermarket bland. This one bites back. It is sold with a rind on, remember that? Nothing like that is on offer in today's mega-store. It's beyond superlatives but can take off the roof of your mouth. If you like your cheese flavoursome, shop here.

Cheddar is the most widely-made cheese in the world and this is the area that lent its name to the product. The fact that most of the processes carried out here are done by hand, makes you realise what a world of difference there is between a traditional dairy and a

cheese factory. The cheese is still matured naturally and the piece
you buy could be well over a year old. Like wine and violins, cheese
really is all the better for keeping.

The Walk

Leave the car park, taking the metalled drive back to the road. This
has a stone wall on one side and a line of beech trees on the other.
Turn left at the end and left again at the crossroads. Cross the road to
the pavement and walk down the hill for some 300m, taking the first
turn right into Back Lane.

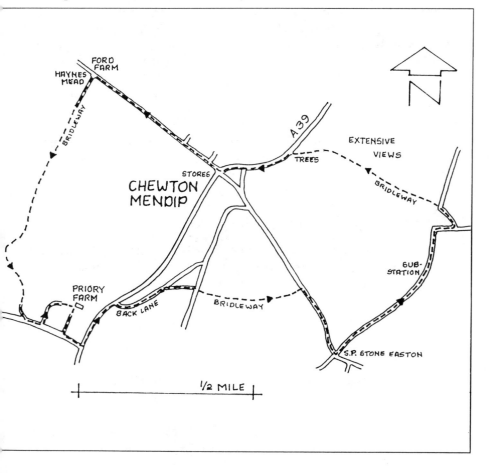

Take the next right, which is Orchard Lane and is little more than a farm road. At the end is a T-junction. Directly ahead is a public bridleway, the route of the walk. This is clearly an historic old green lane that was once used extensively. Small banks line the way, trees behind them. Beyond the trees to the left are pretty views across to the church and village of Chewton Mendip, whilst to the right is a beautiful English farmland scene; small villages and farms – rural England at its best. Should you happen to be walking down here when the church bells are ringing, the glory of the scene is compounded.

The track then starts to drop again as the banks are made up and trees close in, making a little green tunnel. At the end is a road. Turn right and at the crossroads turn left for Ston Easton. Again, there are more views of the village. Pass an electricity sub-station and the road takes a sharp right turn followed by a left turn, which almost takes you back on yourself. As the road then turns another sharp right there is a bridleway directly in front. This is the route of the walk.

You are now walking along the crest of a hill with beautiful views way out on both sides, a patchwork of fields in all directions with the Mendips visible on a clear day. Beyond the ridge, the path curves gently to the left, downhill and into trees, through a gate and back to the road. Here, turn left, down the road into the village and take the first right by the Chewton Mendip Stores.

One thing you may notice about the village is that the name 'Waldegrave' is everywhere. The pub even carries it. Much of the land hereabouts was given to the Waldegrave family in 1553, soon after the Dissolution. There was also a Benedictine priory in the village, but more about that later. The family still own property and live in the area. One of their clan, William, was a minister in the Conservative government of the late 1980s and early 1990s.

Lead was mined in these hills and this rather plain (by Somerset standards) village was home to many of the miners. The church is a fascinating amalgam of architecture, from Norman to fifteenth century. Inside, there is a frid, one of the few remaining sanctuary seats in the country. This is from when a sanctuary was just that; a holy place where debtors and sundry malefactors could seek temporary refuge from their pursuers.

Walk down here for some 400m and look for a stone garage on the left, (paint peeling off the doors) and a house, Haynes Mead. Between these two buildings is a track with a 'Public Bridleway' sign cleverly hidden from view. Turn into the public bridleway opposite Ford Farm and head gently uphill. This is a delightful old wooded lane. Eventually, the lane leaves the wooded area behind and fields appear on each side. This eventually arrives at a road; turn left and then immediately left again, following the sign to Chewton Cheese Dairy. Before you leave the area, there is much more to explore in the dairy. If you are still curious about the actual cheese-making process, there is an informative video that will fill in any blanks.

There are also the remains of an old priory. Only a few bits are left now but the garden is well tended and has a collection of unusual animals and birds. There are owls, squirrels running wild, now almost used to visitors, and some rare farm breeds. The pick of these is probably the English Longhorn cattle. These ancient beef animals, now sadly replaced by continental beasts, are quite magnificent. They were one of the breeds that were exported to the USA to become the basis of their wild west cattle ranch herds.

4. Bruton

Distance:	5 miles.
Start:	The Coffee House, Harlequin Arcade, High Street.
Grid reference:	ST 683347
Parking:	On the High Street or in the car park by the school.

Bruton is a delightful and aged town. Although its origins are Saxon, there is little left from that era. Still, fortunately for those who appreciate beauty and history together, much of the town has remained unaltered for centuries with old buildings aplenty. A measure of this can be noted in the fact that Bruton was the first conservation area in Somerset. The British Council for Archaeology describe it as "...of special importance as regards historic quality." It was on the Roman route to their lead mines in the Mendips. After the Romans left, there are records of a Saxon church around 690 and the town plan of narrow alleys connecting the housing on High Street with the rear lanes, remains. These alleys, incidentally, are known as 'Barton's'.

Prior to the Norman invasion, the town was a borough and had its own mint. Domesday recorded six mills and eighteen plough teams. The reason for such a huge number of mills located in this area is clear to see, even today. The river on which the town's name is based is the Brue. This rises in Selwood Forest, on the slopes of the West Wiltshire Downs just inside the eastern boundary of Somerset and flows some thirty miles to empty into the Bristol Channel at Highbridge.

The Tea Shop

Our selected tea room in Bruton is **The Coffee House** in Harlequin Arcade, just off the High Street. It operates as both delicatessen and bistro; a delightful confusion of tiny tea room with Epicurean items for sale. It is open from 8.30am to 5pm with the wonderfully antique English tradition of a half-day on Thursdays. Note also the date stone over the entrance to The Arcade: 1893.

Before being put to its current use, this Arcade was a garage. In

1998, the town's museum moved in here. Only small and manned by volunteers, it helps to paint a picture of Bruton in times past. With many record books from schools and local businesses, it's a fascinating place and, if used after your walk, will fill in lots of gaps in your knowledge.

The Walk

From the teashop, turn right and take the first alleyway, Amors Barton, to the right. This is steep and very narrow and heads down towards the river. As you walk down here, note the fifteenth century timber framed building.

The walk arrives in a delightful area of cobblestones and walls. Ahead is a ramp that leads to the river where there are stepping-stones. Do not use this; it is just for the pretty view. Turn right down the little road which brings you out alongside the river where there is a delightful miniature castle with a tiny tower. Walk past that, with glorious views across to Bruton School and along a long road past a few garages on the right which serve the big houses on High Street.

The Free Grammar School was founded in 1519 and was the forerunner of what has today become a centre for quality education. There is Kings School, Bruton School for Girls and Sexeys, three fine establishments. Kings School is the one that usually springs to mind when the town is mentioned. It has expanded enormously since its foundation, meeting the needs of discerning parents. The major expansion works took place in the last century, with further work since the war.

This will bring you around again into a green area beside the river. Turn off Back Lane through a metal gate with the bishop's head and yellow footpath signs. This leads you through a little pathway fenced on either side up to a wooden footbridge which goes across the river. This is through an old orchard with some ancient apple trees.

The Brue has been a constant source of grief to Bruton, flooding every time there was more than a little rainfall. This has been greatly alleviated in recent years by the construction of a relief scheme upriver in 1984, which seems to have largely solved the problem.

Up a few small steps, the path the bears round to the left and up another flight of steps. A pretty little seat on the left gives you a view over trees and down to the river. Continue up this path, with more steps, until you join the road. Walk straight across this road up a sharp rise, past an ornate little stone pineapple atop a pillar, and bear right with the road. Some 50m down this lane, as it bears left, directly ahead is a small alleyway with a sign to Plox Green. This is Lovers Walk. Take it and walk to the main road at the far end. Turn left, under the railway bridge and first left along Park Road. Walk up the hill and continue into Park Wall. This is still climbing gently and continues to do so as it passes close to Bruton Dovecote, set atop a rise to the left.

This is a sixteenth century building now under the care of the National Trust. It originally belonged to Bruton Abbey and was given to the NT in 1915 by Henry Hoare Bt. It is unusual in that the square exterior conceals an octagonal interior. Its actual age is of some debate but the consensus seems to be that it was originally a sixteenth century open roofed watch tower, converted some time after the Reformation. A detailed look at the use of pigeons in the domestic economy of yesteryear will be found in Walk 20. From up here, the views across Bruton are simply scintillating.

Bruton dovecote

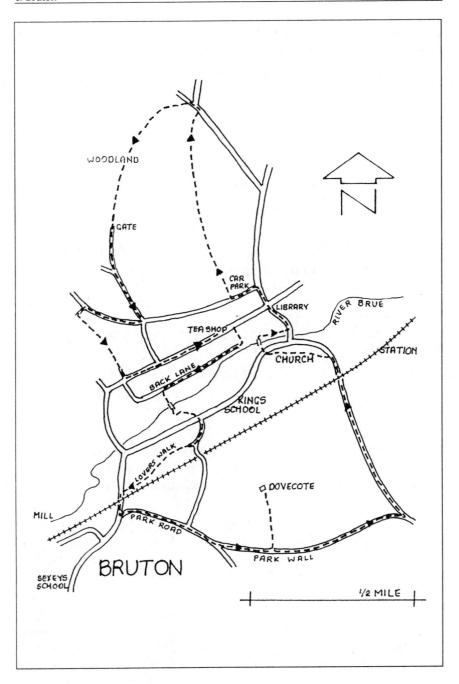

WOODLAND

GATE

CAR PARK

LIBRARY

RIVER BRUE

TEA SHOP

STATION

CHURCH

BACK LANE

KINGS SCHOOL

LOVERS WALK

DOVECOTE

MILL

PARK ROAD

PARK WALL

BRUTON

SEXEYS SCHOOL

N

½ MILE

Carry on along the road to the next junction and turn left. Walk down towards Bruton, passing under the railway again.

There was once an Augustinian priory in Bruton, founded in 1142 which became an abbey in 1510. It was located between the railway and the church, an area now known (unsurprisingly) as Abbey Fields. After the Dissolution, a great house was to be found on the site, owned by the Berkeley family. This survived until about 1786, when it was demolished.

Opposite the turn to the station is a narrow gateway in the wall to the left. This gives entry to the church yard.

St Mary's church is mainly fifteenth century Perpendicular although there is believed to have been a church on this site since Saxon times. There are two towers and a fine chancel, the latter dating from 1743.

Leave the church yard by the opposite exit into Silver Street. Immediately across the road is a small car park and in the left-hand rear corner is an enchanting tiny footbridge over the river. This is a few yards upstream from the stepping stones we saw at the beginning of this walk. Cross the bridge into a small park area and turn right. This leads to Patwell Street; turn left.

The road bridge to the right was damaged in the major flood of 1982 and was the catalyst to the flood prevention scheme. Patwell Pump is housed in a small stone building and was used by the town from about 1900.

Walk up the hill, past the library on the right at the junction and straight up Coombe Street. After 50m, turn left into Higher Backway and take the first right, which is Cheeks Lane, with the car park on the right.

This road soon expires, but continues as a footpath past the left-hand side of old buildings and over a stile before climbing quite steeply. Keeping the woodland to the left, walk over the crest of the hill and down through a field to the bottom left-hand corner. Pass through a gate and the road is re-joined.

Turn left and after a few yards, as the road swings sharp right, there is a farm drive on the left, the entrance to Combe Farm. 10m down here, on the left is a 'Public Footpath' sign. This leaves to the left and up through trees. Almost immediately, there is a split; take the left-hand one. A delightful seat offers a resting place and probably once offered attractive views. Since it was installed, the trees have grown and all you can see is tree trunks.

The path is clearly marked and well used, climbing steeply uphill before passing along the top of a hill which falls away sharply to the right. The walk then leaves the cover of the trees into a slightly wider open glade, which drops down the hill to a brown wooden gate. This leads to a metalled surface. Carry on straight down this lane to a small crossroads where the walk turns right down Tolbury Lane. Follow this as it curves gently to the left and leads alongside the mill leat. Cross a wooden footbridge and carry on, to the left-hand side of a house. Over another bridge with a delightful weeping willow and attractive gardens, the stream is now in the bottom to the right. On the left is the remains of a millpond with a duck farm.

The very names of this area are all that is needed to identify its origins. Coombe Brook, which flows from the north and joins the Brue just below where we walked earlier, was used to power the mill and it is thought that one of the mills mentioned in Domesday was on this site.

Then the walk reaches a narrow lane between two high walls on the edge of the town. This arrives at a T-junction with High Street down Mill Dam; turn left to return to the tea room.

Along High Street, there are aged buildings seemingly beyond count, giving some idea of the wealth that must have existed in this town from the early days. First, wool was processed in Bruton, then cloth weavers came, to be followed by silk weavers and lace makers. All these processes needed power and in those far-off days, it came only from wind or water. Brewing, baking and corn milling have all been found in Bruton over the centuries. Indeed, the town grew rich on wool after weaving was established around 1330.

One man who made his mark away from the town was Hugh Sexey who was an immensely rich financier and Treasurer to Queen Elizabeth I. He bequeathed money on his death in 1615 to establish a charity that would found an almshouse and a place to educate boys. The school on the Yeovil road bearing his name is still operational today, although Sexeys School is an unfortunate name for such an establishment and the butt of many a schoolboy snigger.

Sexeys Hospice on the High Street dates from 1638, although some of it was rebuilt after a disastrous fire in the town in 1731. Its Jacobean Chapel and the Hall are often open to visitors as well as a fascinating stop. A little further along, Priory Court House is basically fifteenth century whilst Chapel Barton House is of a similar date and has been a pub, a silk mill and a church in its time. The frontages to both these buildings are of a much more recent date.

The oldest authenticated building in Bruton is across the road now. Number 31 has a cellar dating from the thirteenth century. The rest is an amalgam of subsequent improvements and alterations and was the local estate office until the 1970s, when it was finally adapted for private use.

There is one remnant of Bruton in those far-off pre-industrial revolution days outside the walk, but within easy reach. Gants Mill is to the right of the A359 Yeovil road. 100m after it passes under the same railway bridge we passed under on the walk. Drive down Gants Mill Lane and follow the road.

This historic working watermill opens from Easter to the end of September on Thursdays from 2pm – 5pm and Bank Holiday Mondays. There are historical artefacts from the Bruton silk industry, corn grinding demonstrations and historical displays over 700 years. It is the best documented mill ever, thanks to the lady in the Hogarth portrait who saved the records.

5. Wells

Distance:	2 miles.
Start:	The Market Place.
Grid reference:	ST 550458
Parking:	In the Market Place.

Wells, the smallest city in England and probably one of the most beautiful. Superlatives roll off the pages of books describing the place and they are all justified. The centre of the city is – and has been for over nine hundred years – the cathedral. It is probably the finest building in the county. Religion in Wells pre-dates this building though. King Ine of Wessex founded a minster church here in the eighth century and Edward the Elder created the diocese of Wells in 909. Here it remained until the end of the eleventh century when the first Norman bishop, John de Villula, moved it to Bath. This remained the diocesan centre until 1244 when it returned to Wells.

Prior to the Norman Conquest, there is scant evidence of any town here. But, by 1180, the city had a Charter and a royal one by 1201 when King John granted it the status of a free borough. Oddly, the cathedral and palace remained outside the borough and was known as St Andrew's Liberty. Subsequently, Wells became the largest place in Somerset with a major wool and cloth manufacturing industry and market. When this trade hit hard times, Wells was less afflicted than others in a similar position. There was real wealth here with the presence of many rich merchants who had made their home in the city to augment the already flourishing ecclesiastical background.

The Tea Shops

For a tea room in Wells, there is an abundance of choice. Two possibilities: the **Good Earth** on Priory Road has an enviable reputation and now manages The Bishop's Buttery in the Palace. Closest to the car park is **Bekynton Brasserie**, a few steps before the entrance to Penniless Porch.

The Walk

Go though the arch known as Bishop's Eye and turn right, walking alongside the moat.

To the left of the archway is a smaller arch. This is known as Penniless Porch. Built by Bishop Bekynton in the mid-fifteenth century, it was a place where the poor could seek alms.

The Bishop's Palace is at the heart of medieval Wells. Moated and fortified, it was the ecclesiastical centre of the city. Construction began in the thirteenth century under Bishop Jocelin and is to this day the residence of the Bishop of Bath and Wells. Most of it is open to visitors, only the fifteenth century North Wing – built by Bishop Beckynton – is excluded. Cross the drawbridge through an arch and you are confronted by a large green area currently acting as a croquet lawn.

Look to the left of the drawbridge, on the wall. There you will see a bell with a rope attached. In the nineteenth century, a bishop's daughter with time on her hands taught the swans to pull on the rope, ringing the bell. The response was food. Descendants of those original swans have learnt

Bishop's Palace Gardens

the trick from their parents and, to this day, they still request feeding this way.

The water for this moat comes from St Andrew's Well, the origin of the city's name. Located to the east of the Palace, there are four springs producing some 100 litres of water a second. As we will see later in the walk, all this water is put to good use, again, courtesy of the church.

Sir Nikolaus Pevsner (1902-83), the German-born authority on English architecture called this place "...the most memorable of all Bishop's Palaces in England." Who are we to argue with the man who produced a series of fifty volumes on *The Architecture of England* between 1954 and 1974.

As the moat ends, walk straight on, past a 'Footpath to Dulcote' sign that leads through a kissing-gate to a metalled path across the field. Strategically placed along this path are a series of seats, offering pleasant views all around but, inevitably, the cathedral dominates the scene.

Work on this edifice was begun around 1180, with Bishop Reginald de Bohun, the man behind it — not that he lived to see it completed. Although it was consecrated in 1239, it was 1508 before all the building work was complete. The stunning West Front is one of the earliest parts, this dating to around 1235. It contains the largest gallery of medieval sculpture in the world. It could almost be described as a stone illustration of Christianity. There are biblical scenes in the lower niches. Looking upwards, you can see kings, bishops, angels and then the twelve apostles and above all, a new statue of 'The Risen Christ'.

Now check out the north transept. Here, you will see a fourteenth century clock. Try to make your visit to this corner coincide with a quarter-hour to see jousting knights across the face. The interior is equally breathtaking. The unique scissor arch was an early solution to sinking foundations of the central tower and was built sometime around 1318.

Over a slight hump, the path continues slightly downhill towards another kissing-gate, down a few steps to a road. Immediately across the road is yet another kissing-gate, this one made from wood, with a footpath sign. This is the walk.

Inside the gate turn left heading straight up a rather steep slope

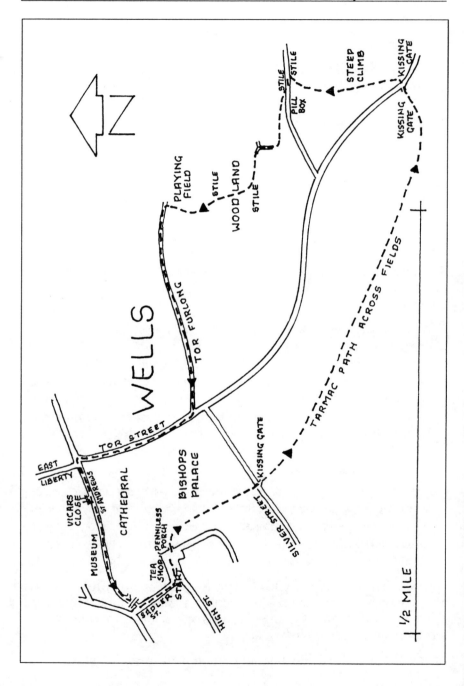

across the field and straight ahead is Pen Hill transmitter mast. Cross the small field to another stile in the hedge opposite beside a stone house. On the left, just beside the hedge as you approach the stile is an old army observation post or pill box. Cross the stile into the lane, turn left and almost immediately opposite is a stone stile with a brass public footpath sign set into the top of the stonework. The whole of the hedge on the left is made of huge blocks of the sort that were used as tank traps in the last war.

The footpath goes diagonally left across the field to the far top corner. At the far end, the path joins a green lane. Turn right and follow this as it circles left. This then opens out into a triangular field with a stile and a way marker in the opposite hedge. This takes the walk into an area of woodland. Follow the path which goes straight ahead. This is quite steep with lots of tree roots and can get quite slippery in wet weather.

Over another stile and follow the path downhill towards the housing, past a playing field and through a wooden gate. Turn left and follow the walk along a wide clear track, Tor Furlong – although it is unmarked at this point. On reaching the main road, turn right up Tor Street. The road swings left and then right, adopting the curious name of East Liberty. At this point, walk straight ahead into St.Andrew Street and take the first right, under the arch, into Vicars Close.

This is the oldest complete medieval street in Europe. It was built in 1363 under the instructions of Bishop Ralph of Shrewsbury as homes for the Vicars Choral. These were clerical assistants and men of the choir, who had previously lived around Wells and were not always as punctual as they should have been. Having them all in one area meant they were easier to control. Over the entrance arch is the Dining Room whilst at the far end of this beautiful street is the chapel and library.

Return to the arch and turn right, into what has now become Cathedral Green. A short distance further along, on the right, is Wells Museum.

The museum started life as a small collection in the cathedral's cloister, being re-located to this building in 1932. Inside, there is a surprisingly wide range of exhibits. Much is concentrated on the Mendips, which is understandable, given the historic discoveries there over the years. The Romans mined lead here and it has been found all over Roman Europe.

Strange to think that, two thousand years ago, lead from these hills would be in use in Pompeii. The city is not neglected though and past and present life is on display. Particularly attractive is a collection of samplers, the earliest of which dates back to 1742.

Continue along Cathedral Green and through the arch at the end, turning left into Sadler Street. At the end, turn left, back into Market Place.

Note the water rushing out from The Conduit. This is relatively new, replacing the original around a century ago. This is the water from the wells. It then washes down the High Street along specially constructed gutters, eventually to join the river Sheppey. As a source of civic cleanliness, it must have been quite something in the days when sewage disposal tended to mean emptying the bucket anywhere that was handy.

Over in the right-hand corner, The Crown is a pub that has existed for many centuries. It was here that William Penn – the Quaker who gave his name to the state of Pennsylvania in the USA – preached from an upstairs window and was promptly arrested.

6. Wedmore

Distance: 4½ miles.

Start: The Borough Venture, The Borough, Wedmore.

Grid reference: ST 436478

Parking: On-street in the village.

This delightful village straddles the B3139 Wells to Burnham Road and sits on the gentle slopes of that east/west watershed with the Axe to the north, the Brue and Huntspill to the south. It positively reeks of age and pretty buildings.

History here can, unusually, be traced back to pre-Norman times. In 878 AD, the Peace of Wedmore was made between the Saxon Alfred the Great and Guthrum the Dane after the Battle of Ethandune in Wiltshire. This was Alfred's first major reply to the Danish invaders after being routed by them early in the year. He retreated to the Athelney Marshes near Langport, raised a new army and attacked.

A quiet corner in Wedmore

Alfred took Guthrum back to Athelney where the latter was baptised. They then repaired to Alfred's *Villa Regis* in Wedmore where the Peace was made. No trace of this house remains but it was probably close to the Manor House, just behind the church.

Subsequently, Aelfred (to give him his proper name) became the scourge of the Danes and ruled all of England that they did not. He died in 899 and his son Edward the Elder continued to harry the Danes, conquering all their Five Boroughs: Leicester, Derby Lincoln, Stamford and Nottingham. After his death in 924, his eldest son Athelstan succeeded to become king of what is generally acknowledged by historians to be, for the first time, a united England.

The Tea Shop

The **Borough Venture** is a licensed coffee shop. Disconcertingly, the front is also a dress shop; yes gentlemen, you have to wade through frocks to reach the tea room. But, be assured, it is well worth the effort. A basic range of eats and drinks are well served in charming surroundings.

There are toilets in the middle of town.

The Walk

Head north, towards Stones Bakery. Take the first right here into The Lerburne.

The Borough is actually the name of this road. It was once the market for Wedmore and, as such was probably once much wider. Opposite the tea room is the Market Cross. This weathered octagonal construction is fourteenth century and once stood further north, opposite the entrance to The Lerburne. Note also Stone's bakery on the corner by the junction. This is another aged structure, part of it dating back to the seventeenth century.

Continue down this lane. Before long, the metalled surface finishes and it becomes something of a track. The route is quite clear, heading off due east. This is quite an easy walk over a hard packed surface that has some use by vehicles and follows the Lerburne, a small stream which gives the impression of being little more than a drainage ditch.

As you get towards the end of this path, looking slightly towards the left you can see the clear conical shape of Brent Knoll (visited in Walk 13) with the Mendips behind. It is now clear that you are walking across a flat plain between two ridges of hills.

One plus of this walk is that it is relatively easy to accomplish, even after wet weather. The number of land drains help to achieve this and there are three to cross on this path.

The track eventually becomes a grass lane and at the end, gives access to a field. Walk straight across this, crossing a wooden sleeper bridge with public footpath sign written in the middle of it. From this point, continue straight down across the next field heading for the river and cross a second footbridge over another drainage channel. Crossing the next field, aim slightly to the right of straight ahead which leads through a sort of gully and out to the river Axe.

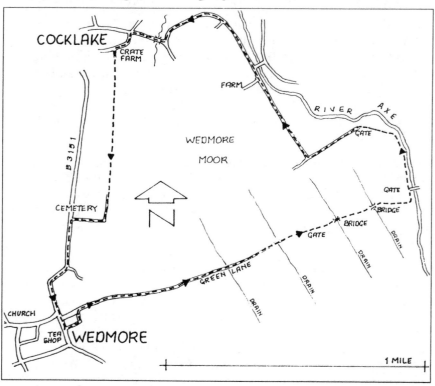

This twenty-five mile long river rises in the Mendips and picks its way
westwards to empty into the Bristol Channel at Uphill, just south of
Weston-Super-Mare.

The path turns left along the banks of the river. There is a padlocked
gate here and a bridge – do not cross the river, stay on the left-hand
bank. On this stretch you are walking between the river on your right
and a row of trees on the left. These are alongside another drainage
ditch. There are herons, mallards, swans and geese to be seen on this
section.

As you approach some electricity wires, a triple stand on telegraph-
type poles, the track bears slightly left, away from the water. This is
now another stone track. As the river attempts to cuddle up to the
path again, the latter is having none of it and turns left, through a
gate. There was originally a kissing-gate on the left here, but it has
been destroyed and is lying in the hedge bottom, in an untidy heap.

The walk then reaches a T-junction in the track. Turn right and at
the next junction, carry straight ahead past a farm and some associated buildings. The river has, by now, returned and is tight in on the
right. This track then reaches a small country lane with a road bridge
to the right. Walk straight ahead, again resisting the temptation to
cross the water, and then sweep around to the left into Cocklake Village. Over a stone bridge, take the left turn between Lane End Farm
and Home Field.

The road swings sharply to the right and a 'Public Footpath' sign on
the left will be encountered, hard by Crate Farm. Follow this clearly
defined track/path with raised ground to the right. The walk is heading pretty well south now and after some 800m passes through gates
with yellow footpath arrows and eventually reaches a metalled surface.

Soon after, the road turns sharp right. Ahead, there is supposed to be
a footpath but, at the time of writing, it appears overgrown and impassable. Should this be re-instated by the time of your visit, follow
it until you reach the lane which formed the outward leg of this
walk, turn right and return to the village. Otherwise, follow the road
up the hill to a main road, turn left and return to the village along
here. **The Borough Venture** tea room will be on the right, just beyond
The Lerborne.

The building dates from the early days of the nineteenth century and is built in Gothic Revival style. Note the original door and windows. The shop windows also match, but are believed to be somewhat newer.

Refreshed, a further exploration of the village can be a rewarding experience. As you return to the village, opposite The Lerborne, take a right turn up Church Street. The church itself is a fascinating old structure. There has been a church on this site since Saxon times but all traces of it have disappeared. The current building is mainly fifteenth century built in the Perpendicular style although several bits of the thirteenth century building can be seen.

The churchyard is a source of great fascination. The fifteenth century Cross was moved to its present location in 1820. There are several venerable yew trees to be seen. Examine the one nearest the cross. It carries a plaque noting that, as the path was being widened in 1853, a pot of 200 silver Saxon coins was discovered. Although most were shipped off to the British Museum in London, the Somerset County Museum at Taunton has retained six of them where they are displayed.

There is also an unusual headstone to the grave of Victor Bracey. He was the son of the local doctor and was killed in 1917, testing a new aeroplane. A carving of the aeroplane is to be found on the cross. Inside the church, the wooden font cover was given in his memory.

Between the church and The Borough is a wonderful accumulation of ancient buildings, all in place well before the planners came up with that phrase that would eliminate any hint of character from which historians of the future may divine pleasure: the building line.

The George Hotel is an eighteenth century coaching inn with a mounting block at the lower end. The bank was built in 1866 as The Assembly Rooms, a quintessentially Victorian institution. Subsequently it saw use as a cinema before becoming a temple to Mammon.

The chemist's shop was once a fashion house. A large tower behind has sadly gone but what remains is elegant nineteenth century Italianite-style, a splendid contrast to others buildings around.

Finally, wonder what this area was once like. In addition to the George, there were pubs in Rosemary Cottage and the post office. Wedmore – like so many rural areas a couple of hundred years ago – must have been awash with beer.

---

7. Glastonbury

Distance: 3½ miles.
Start: Glastonbury Abbey.
Grid reference: ST 499388
Parking: Alongside the abbey in Magdalene St.

If Wells is the most majestic, Glastonbury is the most magical. More wonderful religious ruins, a steep climb preceding unsurpassed views and a choice of several tea rooms as well.

There are so many legends and stories attached to this area that mathematical odds – if nothing else – should make at least some of them true. One story has Glastonbury as the Isle of Avalon – Island of the Blessed Soul in Celtic mythology. This is the last resting place of King Arthur. This was given a degree of credence when twelfth century monks uncovered a Dark Ages burial site. The story handed down is that they discovered a cross together with an inscription: 'Here lies the body of the renowned King Arthur with Guinevere, his second wife in the Isle of Avalon.'

That this area was an island is not in doubt. The Tor itself is 158m (520ft). The Levels were covered extensively by water until the middle ages. The island attracted settlers and prehistoric remains have been found there. The Romans and later the Saxons also settled on the island.

Another visitor of legend was reputed to have been Joseph of Arimathea in 30AD. He brought the Holy Grail with him and placed it in the Chalice Well – visited during the walk. And, if that is not enough, Joseph walked ashore at Wearyall Hill and stuck his staff into the ground. This had been cut from a tree grown from a thorn taken from Jesus' crown. Just what he was doing here and how he chanced upon Glastonbury is not recorded.

The staff took root where it was left and its descendant – known as the Holy Thorn – grows to this day, within the Abbey grounds. Indeed, it was this staff that caused the first Christian establishment to be located here. There are records to prove that this existed by 500AD.

The George and Pilgrim's Hotel

There is another lovely story attached to this staff. During the Civil War, one of Cromwell's soldiers decided that this bush must go. He chopped it down with his sword. Sadly for him, the sword slipped and cut off his leg. The tree we see today is supposed to be a cutting salvaged from the original.

St Patrick was also a one-time visitor to Glastonbury: today's tourists travel in illustrious footsteps. Another Irish saint – Benignus – made a pilgrimage to the town. St Benedict's church was dedicated to this visitor.

The Tea Shop

Although there is a good choice in Glastonbury, our chosen tea room will be the **Abbey Tea Rooms**, directly across the road from the Abbey. You are enjoined to "Come Inside for Good Food and a Warm and Friendly Welcome".

In addition to the usual selection of goodies, you could perhaps fancy hauling a picnic hamper up to the top of the Tor. If that is so, you've come to the right place. This is a wicker hamper (returnable) that includes good quality disposable plates, glasses, crockery and serviettes. Prices start at £5 per person and you can get roast chicken drumsticks, ham and chicken filled finger rolls, mini Scotch egg, fingers of home-made quiche, prawn vol-au-vent, salmon and cucumber sandwiches, crisps and nibbles. Somerset wines are also on offer; which makes a change from Somerset cider. Then, with home-made soup and Somerset cream teas, there is a lot to be said for this delightful establishment.

The Walk

The Abbey Church remains today, standing in thirty-six acres of ground. Tradition has it that this was the first Christian sanctuary in the British Isles. Most of the grounds are open to visitors and, in addition to the monastic remains, King Arthur's Tomb can be seen. This was where the remains were re-interred after their discovery.

Almost one thousand years of Christianity is enclosed within these walls. It was dissolved by Henry VIII in 1539 but had suffered some traumatic times even before that. In 1184, the whole building was destroyed by fire. It was subsequently rebuilt and redeveloped, work that was still

on-going at the Dissolution. Most of the extensive remains are thirteenth and fourteenth century. The Abbot's Kitchen is probably the
most complete building on site; apart from the Abbey House, which is not
open to visitors. This will be encountered later; from a different angle.

Leave the Abbey and turn right, following the main road around to the right and into High Street.

Note the Victorian Market Cross standing at the foot of High Street.
This elegant piece of stonework is just one aspect of this part of town
that is so fascinating. There are many other historic buildings, the
George and Pilgrim's Hotel having been founded in the thirteenth century. Much of this part of town is designated a Conservation Area. A
couple of doors further up is the real classic building of Glastonbury. The
Tribunal was believed to have originally been a courthouse. Today, it
houses the tourist information office and The Lake Village Museum.

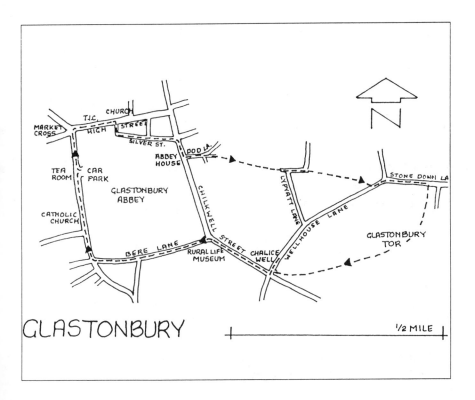

You will also get a flavour of the mystic air about this place. Look around you. There cannot be another town in the country with a greater percentage of young hirsute males, each with a lurcher in tow. Old Volkswagen Caravettes, often decorated with astrological signs are also here in great profusion.

Still not convinced? Check out the shop names. 'The Archangel Gabriel Soul Therapy Centre' provides tools for personal and planetary assertion. Magic shops, stocking a stunning variety of gewgaws are more in evidence than food shops. You don't eat in Glastonbury, you indulge in astral feasting!

Walk up High Street as far as the parish church of St John the Baptist. Opposite, a narrow alleyway marked 'Hanover Square leading to Silver Street'. Turn right into this and continue to the top of Silver Street. Turn right, and after 200m, take a left into Dod Lane.

As you make the left turn, note the Abbey House entrance. This wonderful old building is now in use as a conference centre and retreat.

Some 100m along, this splits. A road leaves to the right, followed by a left-hand bend. At this point, a small cul-de-sac with 'Private Road – No Parking' sign. Walk into here and at the top, a gate leads into a field. This path then continues for 300m, starting to climb until it meets a narrow lane arriving from the right; continue straight ahead. 50m along, the road turns sharp left and a path continues up a short slope to a gate with stile alongside; take this.

When this path reaches the next road – Wellhouse Lane – turn left, up the hill. 300m up here, a clearly marked – and well used – track leaves to the right. This will take you to the summit of Glastonbury Tor.

The views from the top of this conical shaped hill are outstanding. It has also long been a place of Christian pilgrimage. The tower on the summit is all that remains of the fourteenth century St Michael's church.

Carry on down the other side of the Tor, following the clearly delineated path. At the bottom, the path arrives back at Wellhouse Lane, quite close to the bottom. Turn right here to visit the Chalice Well.

Apart from the supposed resting place of the Holy Grail, Chalice Well has an ancient tradition of providing healing waters. 25,000 gallons

(113,000 litres) flow each day and the water is a constant 52°F (11°C). Accordingly, at one time it was in great demand as a spa. Those days are now gone but the water has a mystical effect on the area. The water can still be a rusty red colour, thus providing the alternative name of Blood Spring. This has far less to do with the Holy Grail; more the ironstone in the ground hereabouts.

Further evidence of the alternative healing and lifestyle to be found in Glastonbury is evidenced by the building just below the Well. Berachah House offers colour healing, Auro Soma Reading, Auro Soma Massage and Hand Painted Silks. Well, that's one thing we can all understand.

Walk to the bottom of the hill and turn right into Chilkwell Street, then take the second left, which is Bere Street. Here, the fourteenth century Abbey Barn contains The Somerset Rural Life Museum.

This tells the story of rural life in Somerset in the nineteenth century. The reconstructed farm buildings surrounding the courtyard contain displays illustrating the techniques and tools of farming. Learn how willow growing became big business, how the drainage of the Levels resulted in extensive peat workings and discover about mud horse fishing. What on earth is that? It's a delightfully offbeat activity; exactly what, is a secret for you to uncover.

Walk down Bere Lane.

This is the least edifying stretch of this walk. The road and buildings surrounding it have all the grace and elegance of Darmoor prison.

Turn right at the bottom along Fishers Hill which runs into Magdalene Street, past the Catholic Church and the tea room on the left-hand side, opposite the car park.

8. Street

Distance:	5 miles.
Start:	The Crispin Centre, High Street, Street.
Grid reference:	ST 488367
Parking:	Several car parks in the immediate area.

Street likes to think of itself as the largest village in England; a claim disputed by several other places. Nevertheless, it is a delightful place, owing much to the industrial revolution. Prior to this, it was nothing more than a collection of small houses on a ridge above the Somerset Levels, at the other end of a causeway which crossed the Brue towards Glastonbury. Stone quarrying and agriculture were the main ways to eke out a living. Leather tanning was also carried out and it was here that a young man, James Clark, was apprenticed at his brother's tannery.

Clarke's Village,

Looking at ways of using offcuts from sheep skins, he persuaded local shoemakers to make slippers. In 1825, he formed a company with his brother that was to become world-renowned for shoe making, still with its headquarters in the village.

The Tea Shop

Our tea room in Street is located in Crispin Hall, a listed building named after the patron saint of shoemakers. It was opened by John Bright on October 12th 1885, when William Clark – of the shoe family – decided to improve the quality of his workers education.

The Mad Hatter Café is a no-frills establishment offering an excellent range of basics; Welsh rarebit, eggs on toast, hamburgers, soups and light lunches. Prices are quite reasonable with a cup of tea costing 35p, coffee 65p. It's a no-smoking place, open from 9am to 5pm during the week and on Sundays during the summer. Also within this building, you will see an indoor market, advice centre, art gallery and other shops.

The Walk

Leave the Crispin Centre, turn right and right again almost immediately into Leigh Road. Continue straight ahead at the first crossroads where Vestry Road and Hind Hayes Lane arrive from the right and left respectively, and follow Leigh Road as it bears gently round to the right and straightens up before reaching a T-junction. Ahead, to the left of a farm building, a couple of steps and a narrow crush lead into a public footpath (signposted). Follow this path across the fields towards a small stone construction. Exit the field through another crush to the left of this building.

> This turns out to be a redundant school. Redundant for its original purpose maybe, but it still echoes to the happy sound of children as the Overleigh Play Group now operate from here.

Turn right along the lane and turn left at the road junction. Just before the corner you will pass Tumbledown cottage which is a complete misnomer, today at least. Continue along Overleigh for some 300m until the right turn, which is Middle Brooks. Take this and after 175m turn left into Gooselade. This is a cul-de-sac. Turn immediately right and at the end, in the left-hand corner is a track between two houses that crosses a stile and heads out straight across a field, climbing slightly as it does so.

Pass close to the pole carrying wires and through a gate at the far end. This in turn leads to another narrow field. In the top left-hand corner is the exit that brings the walk into a narrow lane. Turn right. Walk down this lane, past the youth hostel entrance to a large oak tree on the left.

Here a bridleway leaves, uphill again. Eventually, after some 300m, this bridleway leads into an area of common land a few metres from a road. Turn right here and follow the track that runs along the top edge of the trees. This runs parallel to the road for almost a mile before emerging from the trees, crossing to the left-hand side of the road and continuing amid more trees.

The path then leaves the woodland, crosses a stile and enters more open countryside, along the crest of Walton Hill with views over the Somerset Levels. Some of this land is in the care of the National Trust.

It was here, on Ivythorne Hill at Marshall's Elm, that thirty of the Duke of Monmouth's rebellious army were hanged for their part in the uprising of 1695. More details of this event are noted in Walk 14. This is an Environmentally Sensitive Area (ESA) where government (MAFF) is working with farmers to conserve and enhance characteristic landscapes, wildlife habitats and historic features. Those participating in the ESA scheme are encouraged to manage their land in ways that benefit the environment. The Levels are internationally renowned for their bird life and also contain sites of historic importance featuring ancient settlements and timber trackways preserved in the peat.

Continue along the path passing a car park and the brow of another hill from where the truncated remains of a white painted windmill hove into view. On the down slope is a stile on the right allowing you to regain the road at the point where the narrow Veal Lane leaves to the right, downhill.

This executes a sharp right bend after 400m followed by an equally sharp left-hand bend. At this point, a track leaves towards the right through a metal gate. After 100m along the green lane, there is a gateway on the left. Although unsigned, this is a public footpath with a section to the left of the gate to climb over. Follow the track until it reaches a lane and turn right and walk for some 100m to a stile on the left, well concealed by the hedgerow. Cross this, taking a sight on the distant Glastonbury Tor for your direction.

Pass through an open gateway at the far end, keeping the hedge generally to your right shoulder. As the hedge turns right, the walk continues towards a tiny opening that leads through a hedge into the woodland and a well-beaten track. The trees then close in and the path becomes almost a tunnel. Drop down a small slope and cross a stream with a little pond on the left, over another stile into a field. Cross this and then go over another stile and into a narrow lane.

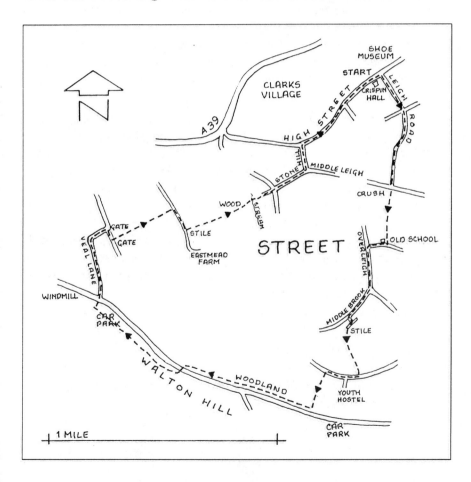

This is a rough track, and carries straight on across the road into Stone Hill. Walk down there until the junction with Middle Lea and bear left with Stone Hill. Follow this road to the next junction and turn right into High Street and back to the Crispin Centre.

Although this is the end of the walk, there is much, much more to see. As mentioned, Street is essentially a product of the industrial revolution and does not have a great supply of venerable buildings.

Millfield School, one of our better known private schools is based here at the east end, off Somerton Road. This draws pupils from all around the globe, such is its reputation.

Across the road from Crispin Hall are Farm Road and the oldest part of the Clark empire. This has been converted to The Shoe Museum. With free admission, it houses a collection of footwear from Roman times to the present day. Shoe machinery and artefacts associated with the industry are displayed together with old documents and photographs. Fascinating.

A little further along Farm Road is the entrance to Clarks Village. This is a simply huge retail complex with footwear shops (surprisingly!) and over fifty other retailers which covers pretty well anything you could want or need. There are plenty of bargains too. Well-known names offering discontinued lines, seconds and samples pull in shoppers from miles around. It was the first purpose-built, factory-shopping scheme in the UK and is located in a picturesque setting with restaurant, picnic area and children's play area. It also holds The Village Pottery which sells some attractive earthenware. There are regular demonstrations of pottery making as well as the chance to get on the potter's wheel and demonstrate your skills – if any!

Around the village, Sharpham Park Farm was the birthplace of Henry Fielding (1707-54). Best known as the author of *The History of Tom Jones, a Foundling* his satirical writing was responsible for the passing of the Theatrical Licensing Act of 1737. He also worked with his half-brother John to form the Bow Street Runners, an early attempt at policing London's streets.

9. Langport

Distance:	3½ or 4 miles.
Start:	Huish Bridge Car Park. Heading west on the A371 towards Langport, pass St Mary's church and turn left at the end. Take the first right down a narrow lane.
Grid reference:	ST 424264
Parking:	At the start.

Although headed 'Langport', this walk is along the Levels to the south of the town. Its presence in the title is a useful adjunct to locating the walk which starts at the bottom of a nondescript lane on the southern edge of town.

The Tea Shop

The Stable Tea Room, found at the furthest extremity of the walk has a delicious range of cakes, drinks, pasties and cream teas. As with so many of our tea stops in Somerset, the cakes are all home-made.

The Walk

Leave the little car parking area, heading north-west towards the church and Langport, along the right-hand side of the river Parrett. This leads to a bridge which takes the walk over the second stream to the right. Then, across a field and over another footbridge and a stile, along the clearly marked path up a steep stony track with a very pretty stone house to the left. At the top is a road where the walk turns right. Stay on this road and bear left to reach the very beautiful Huish Episcopi church on the left.

The very name of this area – Huish Episcopi – gives an indication of its religious connections. An episcopate being the office (or see) of a bishop. The bishop in question here was the bishop of Bath and Wells. The patron of this living is the archdeacon of Wells.

The building itself has retained its Norman doorway, which is twelfth century. The church was destroyed by fire in the fourteenth century and the terracotta colour of this surviving stonework is presumed to be due to that inferno. Perhaps the most outstanding feature (literally) is the tower. This reaches some 30m (99ft) into the Somerset sky and is quite magnificent. It houses a peal of eight bells, which have been added over the years, the most recent were two hung in 1957.

Rejoin the walk along to the main road and join it, continuing ahead. Pass the war memorial and on to the **Rose and Crown**, a free house with a pleasant garden and plenty of seats outside. It is open all day on Friday, Saturday and Sunday serving fine teas and coffee, light snacks and all sorts of home-made food. During the week, hours are restricted to lunch time and evening sessions.

The ancient Rose and Crown pub at Huish Episcopi

It is a fascinating old building with thatched roof and arched windows – very episcopal. There are lots of intriguing separate rooms including one known as the Men's Kitchen and a lovely big garden with a children's play area.

Turn around, walk back up the road until Court Field is reached.

Turn left and at the end, pass through a kissing-gate, heading off across the field to another kissing-gate in the bottom corner. Through this gate, turn right and follow the track until you reach a metalled road. Follow this to a T-junction and turn left. Follow this minor road – which is also part of a cycle route organised by the county – and cross two bridges, the first over a drain, the second crossing the river Yeo.

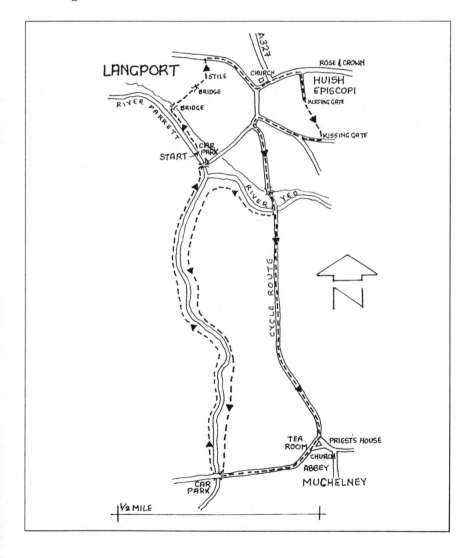

Once known as the Ivel, this twenty-four mile long river rises in Dorset and gives its name to the town of Yeovil through which it passes. It joins the Parrett close to the car park where this walk started.

There is now a choice of routes. One is waterside but longer, the other stays with the road, which can get busy at times. Both meet at Muchelney.

Route One: Continue along the road, crossing further drains, to the next junction, which is by the church in Muchelney.

Route Two: Turn right immediately beyond the bridge and follow the footpath along the raised banks of the Yeo. At its confluence with the Parrett, turn left and continue to the next road-bridge. Leave the river, turn left and walk 400m to Muchelney.

The church at Muchelney is St Peter and St Paul. This early fifteenth century building has a remarkable painted ceiling depicting somewhat buxom female angels; attired in Tudor dress. As with Glastonbury, this area was once an island and the remains of Muchelney Abbey are the second oldest in the county after Glastonbury – see Walk 7. It was founded around 697 by King Ine of Wessex and survived until the Reformation. This was a Benedictine establishment where the cloisters and abbot's lodgings are well preserved. They are in the care of English Heritage.

Across the road, The Priest's House is also very ancient. Its construction is believed to have started around 1308 and it was originally built as a single hall with a parlour, serice and solar room. It was provided as a home for priests who served the church across the way. Gothic windows are particularly impressive and the place is open to visitors. Its owners, The National Trust, let it to a tenant.

Time also for the tea stop. Just off the main road by the church is the Almonry, a place where alms were once distributed. Now, refreshment is offered to weary travellers. The Stable Tea Room, across from the church, is fashioned as a stable with a wonderfully uneven floor, hay racks, individual partitions and an external sitting area overlooking the pollarded willows alongside the small stream. Also in the block is an architect together with an art school and gallery.

Leave Muchelney heading west along the road to Curry Rivel (the way that Route Two arrived at the village). On reaching the river Parrett, cross and turn right. Follow the west bank of the river. This is marked 'Footpath to Huish Bridge.'

In some respects, the Somerset levels are very similar to the Fens of East Anglia: height above sea level, lots of rivers and drains. But there the similarity ends. Whereas the fens are acres and acres, miles and miles of nothing, the Levels are intimate, small fields of grass with hedges instead of prairies full of wheat. There are also trees here where a tree in the fens almost qualifies for a preservation order.

At the first bridge you reach, turn right, cross it and return to the car park – the end of the walk.

10. Montacute

Distance:	3 miles.
Start:	The Square, Montacute.
Grid reference:	ST 498169
Parking:	In the Square.

A walk of some contrasts, involving a quite sharp uphill section, one that is rewarded by scintillating views over the whole county.

The Tea Shop

The tea room for this walk is thoroughly offbeat. It's housed in The Montacute TV, Radio & Memorabilia Museum on South Street.

Owned and run by Alan and Marcia Hicken, this is a wonderful tribute to yesteryear. It's a thoroughly eclectic collection of household and domestic appliances, early radios (of which there are some 400), film, television, pop, children's books, toys, old advertising signs, tins and packaging plus a whole lot more. There is a collection of books and games with a television tie-in. Remember Champion the Wonder Horse, The Lone Ranger and The Men From U.N.C.L.E.? All of them had annuals and they represent but a few of the 1,000+ on display. In all, an extraordinary collection and a cheery set-up.

The tea room itself is open from Easter to the end of October. The hours are 10am to 5.30pm, Sundays from 11am to 6pm. Everything from tea to a good meal is available, much of it home-made. This can range from the ubiquitous cream teas through to a good savoury menu with vegetarian choices. The fruit pies and that west country speciality; apple cake, come into the 'home-made' category and are quite excellent.

The zany nature of this set-up is evidenced in the tea room. Examine the Alice in Wonderland Collection housed in the Mad Hatters Tearoom. Clearly if you can't beat 'em, join 'em. If the main museum is Alan's pride and joy, this is Marcia's response. There is china, books, puzzles, dolls, in fact, anything remotely to be connected with Alice. Outside, there is a tea garden with a play area for tots.

Montacute House

And, if this is not enough, the listed Georgian property also offers bed and breakfast. At the time of writing, a double room costs from £30 a night with continental breakfast, an extra £4 for full English.

The Walk

Turn right from the Square along South Street and at the first sharp left-hand bend, take the lane on the right – Townsend – by the Stax Saddlery.

If you need any more evidence that Montacute is essentially a collection of glorious stone buildings, this area will provide it. In addition, on the right, there is a lovely view over to the church and Montacute House, both of which we visit later in the walk.

The walk is now a gentle climb up a small country lane.

Strip lynchetts – medieval farming terraces – can be seen from here, clearly cut into the hillside. These allowed farmers to plough the steep slopes of the hill.

After 400m, there is a track on the right. Hard by this is a stile in the hedge and a sign indicating the way to Batemoor Barn. Cross this and walk parallel with the road which is on the other side of the hedge, continuing uphill.

At the next stile, do not cross but turn right and walk alongside the fence to another stile. Cross this one and turn right – downhill – to a gate. Pass through this and, keeping the fence to the right, walk to the next stile. After crossing this stile, turn left towards the trees.

The walk now starts to climb again as it enters Hedgecock Hill Wood. Turn left at the first meeting of tracks and continue over one stile before meeting another. Cross this and continue uphill, over the remains of a wall.

The path narrows, winds and undulates before reaching a really steep section. At the end of this grassy section by some large boulders, a signpost indicates the right-hand turn back to Montacute; follow this and turn right – uphill – at the next junction.

There is a short diversion at this junction. Turn left and after 200m left again up a flight of steps, then right up a very steep – but mercifully short – path to a road with **The Prince of Wales** pub. This is a flower-covered free house with delightful views out over the valley. There is a road that circles this area, part of Ham Hill Country Park. This is some 400m round and there is a play area and toilets to be discovered here.

> The Country Park covers over 60ha and is some 90m above sea level. It is managed by South Somerset District Park although the land actually remains in private ownership. There was an Iron Age fort up here and quarrying for the glorious golden stone seen hereabouts was carried out for centuries. Return by the same route to the junction to continue the walk.

This is a twisty track through woodland. Follow the track, keeping the fields to your left as the walk starts to descend. Some 200m along, a flight of steps on the left, lead to a lower path. Follow this for some 900m until the path meets another. Bear left here and pass through a gateway. By now, the path has developed into a quite distinctive lane. Some 100m along, the lane turns left. Here, there is an optional diversion up to the top of St Michael's Hill. To continue the main walk, go to *MAIN ROUTE*.

Opposite are a few steps up to a kissing-gate. A signpost indicates 'National Trust – Footpath Only'. This path is across a grass field to start with, before developing into a well-made one, which winds round the hillside, climbing steeply, until it reaches the summit. After admiring the wonderful views from up here, re-trace your steps down to the kissing-gate.

It was on this hill in about 1035 that a crucifix carved in black flint was discovered. This was eventually taken to Waltham Abbey in Essex where it is reputed to have been used to cure King Harold's paralysis. This is why his battle cry at Hastings was "Holy Cross".

There was a castle built on this summit soon after the Normans landed but all traces of it have now disappeared. The tower we see today was a folly/observatory (depending on whose interpretation of history is to be believed), built in 1760 by Sir Edward Phelips who lived at Montacute House.

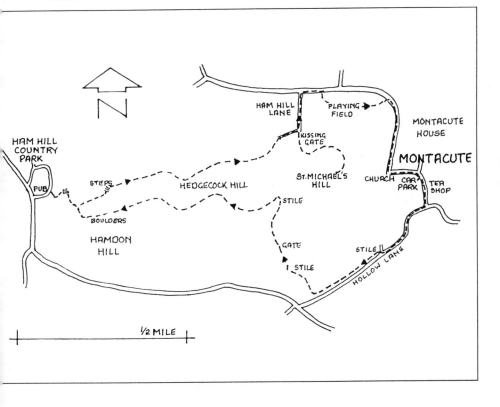

MAIN ROUTE: Continue down the lane to a main road and turn right. Some 100m after a road junction on the left – opposite a bus shelter – is the entrance to a sports field on the right. Rather than follow the road, walk through this area which eventually leads back to the road beyond the children's play area. Walk through the village along Bishopston to the church of St Catherine, opposite The Kings Head.

There was a church here in Saxon times. Whether it was on this particular spot is not clear. What is known is that the cross discovered on St Michael's Hill, was reputed to have been found after the sexton had a dream about it. If there was a sexton then, there was a church as well.

The present building was started in Norman times and is believed to have been a chapel in the burial grounds of the Clunaic priory. Subsequently, it became the parish church whilst the priory church disappeared – along with the priory – at the Dissolution in 1539.

Much of the building was renewed in 1870 and, unlike many such efforts in Victorian times, does not seem to have had too bad an effect on it. The interior has the usual collection of memorials to local landowners – in this case, the Phelips – and their family pew is in the south transept.

Outside in the churchyard to the south, it is possible to see some remnants of the priory. The battlemented gatehouse is the principal – and thoroughly imposing – remnant although a few associated buildings also exist. They all form part of Abbey Farm, are privately owned and not open to visitors.

Turn right from the church and follow the road back to the car park. The tea room is across the road.

Opposite the car park is the entrance to Montacute House. This National Trust building is a truly superb Elizabethan mansion, built for Sir Edward Phelips in the last years of the sixteenth century. The mason responsible was one William Arnold, a Somerset man. His was the skill that created a number of other fine buildings around the country. Perhaps most notable was Wadham College in Oxford.

Sir Edward was a famous public figure of his day. He was an MP who would become Speaker of the House in 1604 and made the opening speech for the prosecution when Guy Fawkes was tried for treason. The

'H' shaped ground plan of the House includes many Renaissance features and a second floor gallery which is 44m long.

There is some fine furniture from the seventeenth and eighteenth centuries and some Elizabethan and Jacobean portraits from the National Portrait Gallery. The gardens are exquisite with many beautiful old roses.

Montacute House was sold out of the Phelips family a century or so ago and had several tenants before being given to the NT in 1931. One such was Lord Curzon. He was a Viceroy of India from 1898 until 1905 and then Foreign Secretary from 1918 to 1924. He made his home here from 1915 until his death in 1925.

Elsewhere in the village, there are some delightful houses, all built of Ham Hill stone. The cottages on South Street were once used by workers in the glove trade, an important source of employment a couple of hundred years ago.

One unusual aspect of this village, which ensured that it stands out from others we visit, is the almost total lack of thatch. There is an abundance of this throughout Somerset; in Montacute, only one is immediately visible.

The aged aspect of the place, with few recent buildings, makes Montacute quite a draw for film makers. The most recent was Sense and Sensibility, Jane Austen's epic story about two sisters which starred Emma Thompson and Hugh Grant amongst a wonderful cast.

11. Hatch Beauchamp

Distance:	3½ miles.
Start:	The Hatch Pub, Hatch Beauchamp.
Grid reference:	ST 302205
Parking:	On street locally.

This pleasant walk through deepest Somerset offers the chance to inspect the remains of thoroughly unsuccessful canal. Considering the lack of heavy industry in this county, there was an abundance of navigable waterways; as we will see later.

The Tea Shop

The Farthings, although a hotel, does a rather good line in teas: traditional and *very* English. The building is a Georgian country house and the owners have made a conscious attempt to re-create that atmosphere. Tea on the front lawn is elegance personified.

The Walk

Walk down the hill, signposted Taunton. After 300m, a narrow lane on the right leaves under an old railway bridge.

> This was the railway built to connect Taunton and Chard. It also led to the demise of the Chard canal, which we will meet shortly.

Follow this quiet narrow lane past a few houses initially before reaching empty countryside. At the end of this lane is a main road. Turn right here and after 30m, right again through a metal gate, just before the farm and the pub. Walk up the farm track. On the left are the remains of the Chard Canal.

> Schemes to provide water transport to Chard were first proposed 1769, when Robert Whitworth surveyed a line from the river Parrett to Seaton, on the south Devon coast. This was part of his survey of possible links between the English Channel and Bristol.

After a succession of proposals, it was in 1821, that another survey, this time employing James Green, was arranged. His recommendation was for a tub boat canal. Green's scheme was eventually accepted in 1834. The original plan was for two boat lifts and two inclined planes, but the concept of boat lifts on the Grand Western Canal near Taunton had caused so much trouble that they were dropped; as was Green. His successor, Sydney Hall, settled for four inclined planes.

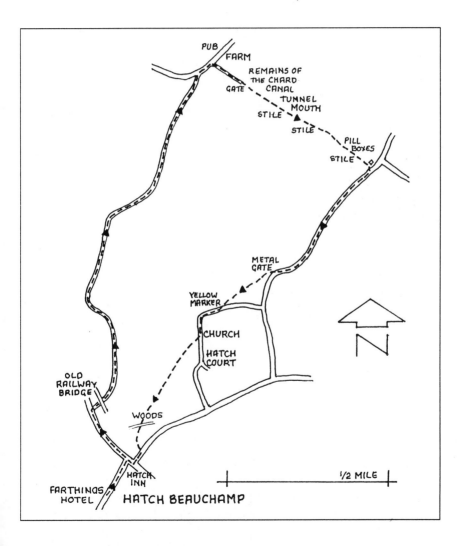

Work started on Midsummer's Day 1835. The canal was built 13.5 miles long, and needed to rise 231ft before reaching Chard. In addition to the planes, three tunnels and two locks were needed. Because of the uneven ground, much of the canal had to be constructed either in cuttings or on long embankments and two aqueducts were built to cross roads.

Work proceeded very slowly, and it was not until May 1841, that the section from Creech St Michael to Ilminster was completed. A Grand Opening Ceremony was instituted that saw a boat laden with canal worthies depart for Ilminster. What happened thereafter is something of a mystery. It is believed that the party failed to reach their destination, the cause seeming to have been the two inclined planes at Thornfalcon and Wrantage. Whether they were even complete is a moot point. The earliest record of a through passage is July 27th that year.

Chard was finally reached in May 1842, but the canal never carried the amount of freight needed to make it viable. A mere 25 years later, the railway company bought and closed it.

This track is used by farm vehicles and livestock, and can get extremely muddy. It leads to a stile. Cross this and the lane instantly improves underfoot. The walk is now grassy, not suffering the constant attrition of farm use.

The slope on the left was The Wrantage Inclined Plane. This lifted the canal some 9m and the basin at the bottom still holds water. An inclined plane was a method of allowing boats to move from one water level to another without the use of locks. A slope was constructed connecting the two levels and some form of winding gear fitted. There were several methods used over the years, the most popular being a waterwheel driving a capstan around which a rope was fitted. This was connected to the tub boat at the bottom and it was dragged to the top where it re-floated. Because of the limited power available, tub boats were built small and operated in trains pulled by a horse. Wheels were fitted on the base.

On the left, just beyond the stile is the start of Crimson Hill tunnel.

At 1646m long, this was the major civil engineering task on the canal. It was built without a towing path and just wide enough for one tub boat and must have been dauntingly claustrophobic. Examination from the end will reveal stonework in extremely fine condition, a reflection on the quality of the tradesmen who built it. This length is still in water, with the trees and undergrowth making a delightfully sylvan scene.

Wartime remains; observation point on Crimson Hill

The path climbs steeply as it passes under a stand of trees. You can pause here and look back over the view with the tunnel entrance below and Somerset laid out in front of you. A thoroughly pleasant location.

The path then reaches a gate, which carries a notice advising you that your path follows the red topped posts. What posts? Over a new stile, the path enters a small field. Here, continue straight ahead, very slightly to the right of the scrubby bushes in front of you. On the top of here are two wartime pill boxes, set down into the hill. The exit is immediately behind them. Again, turn and enjoy the superb view from up here.

Cross another new wooden stile into a narrow path alongside a hedge, which is the garden belonging to a house here. This leads out into a country lane; turn right. Walk along this lane for some 800m and, as the road sweeps left, on the right is an entrance with a large metal gate. To the left of this entrance is a 'Public Footpath' sign. Follow this across a field, walking in the direction of the church tower. Between the trees, on the edge of the drive you are approaching is a post with a yellow footpath sign. Turn right and follow the drive down towards Hatch Court, a fine stone building.

This wonderful Palladian mansion was built in Bath stone by Thomas Prowse of Axbridge in 1750. It is still in the same family, the current owners – and fifth generation – being Dr. and Mrs Robin Odgers.

This really is a delightful place to stop off for a while. The entrance hall is particularly grand with a cantilevered stone staircase and Ionic pillars. There is a good collection of English and French furniture and paintings from the last two centuries.

The semi-circular China Room houses porcelain and glass and a small military museum in the next room commemorates the founder of the last privately raised regiment The Princess Patricia's Canadian Light Infantry, Brigadier Hamilton Gault. He was a local MP and great uncle of the present owner.

Outside, the gardens won the Taunton Deane Historic Garden Restoration Award in 1995 and offer a walled kitchen garden, a superb display of roses and a clematis wall. The surrounding parkland is home to a herd of fallow deer.

One special aspect of a visit to this place is that tours are conducted by members of the family, adding a personal dimension that most other places of this type do not. The Gardens and Park are open throughout the summer months but the House times are somewhat limited. Details can be discovered by calling 01823 480120.

When you reach the church, a path leaves to the right, opposite the car parking area. Walk down this path with a hedge to the left, a field and wire fence to the right. Through a wooded area, a junction is reached. Cross straight over, following the marked Public Footpath. This reaches a small road where the walk turns right, down towards **The Hatch** pub.

For the tea room, turn left and **The Farthings** is 300m along on the right.

12. Maunsel

Distance:	2½ miles.
Start:	Maunsel Canal Centre, Banklands, North Newton, Bridgwater, Somerset TA7 0DH. Tel: 01278 663160.
Grid reference:	ST 308297
Parking:	In the car park, across the road from the canal.

Still finding pleasure and tranquillity around water, this walk includes a length of the Bridgwater and Taunton Canal, almost the furthest west you can get on a navigable waterway in England.

The Tea Shop

Our tea room is at the Maunsel Canal Centre. The owners, Sylvia and Tony Rymell were at the forefront of the campaign to restore the navigation for boating use. The tea room opened soon after the canal itself had been restored to boats although the towing path has been open to walkers for many years, after similar restoration work was carried out.

The Bridgwater and Taunton Canal was originally conceived as part of a waterway link between Bristol and the English Channel at Exeter, thus avoiding the then perilous passage around Lands End. At this time, early in the nineteenth century, shipwrecks were almost an everyday occurrence in those treacherous waters. The toll of lives lost around the Cornish coast in vessels powered by – and at the mercy of – the wind, was quite horrific.

After years of bickering over a route, the length between Bridgwater and Taunton opened in 1827. Another section was already built: the Grand Western Canal around Tiverton (Devon). And there the thing stood. In 1838, a small canal that could be used by tub boats (see Walk 11 for a more detailed description of this peculiar form of transport) was built, linking the eastern end of the GW's section at Lowdwells with the B & T in Taunton (see Walk 14). However, the southern extension to Exeter was never completed.

This section lasted a scant 30 years. Railway competition, in the shape of the Bristol and Exeter Railway, stole the trade and then bought out and closed the tub boat length. Inevitably, this had an adverse effect on the B & T, although the railway did invest money to improve the dock at Bridgwater. When the Great Western Railway took over, their particular brand of tender loving care (total neglect) was soon evident. The last tolls on the B & T were collected in 1907 and the line just quietly festered away.

The canal remained moribund until the enthusiasm for restoration up country was mirrored there. It took twenty years of effort from volunteer groups, BW and local authorities before the complete re-opening was celebrated in 1994. This involved fund-raising, organising campaigning events and publicising the amenity value of this waterway. As mentioned earlier, Tony and Sylvia were at the forefront of this activity and were delighted to be offered the tenancy of this place, the only remaining lock cottage on the B & T.

Because of their remoteness from civilisation, canal companies throughout the land were forced to provide housing for their employees, especially the lock keepers. That very remoteness then worked against many of these fine old buildings as the canals became disused, abandoned and falling into total ruin. The buildings they provided followed a similar course. This was before the age

On the Bridgwater and Taunton Canal

when many people's idea of Utopia was a remote canalside cottage with no water, electricity or sewage system.

The Tea Shop

The tea room – which is open during the summer only – offers teas, cream teas, scones, toasted teacakes and a cake selection. Soft drinks, confectionery and ice cream are also on sale in the shop, along with canal books and magazines, souvenirs and painted canal ware. There is also plenty of information about this canal, tables and chairs outside and a pretty garden area by Maunsel Lock. You can also take a boat trip from here – again, only during the summer months.

The Walk

Turn left at the entrance to the car park, cross the canal and turn right, pick up the canal towing path and turn right, back under the bridge.

Close to the lock, you will see a plaque, which is part of the Somerset Space Walk. This one represents 'Mars', the planet most like earth with 24-hour days, as well as seasons, mountains, plains and valleys. It once had water and possibly air. Secrets of the planet and its history are continuing to be revealed. But why this, here?

The Somerset Space Walk was conceived by Pip Youngman and executed with the able assistance of the canal staff. She worked out that, at a scale of 530,000,000:1, the length of the B & T was the size of our universe. So working outwards from the sun, a representation of each planet is to be found along the towing path at a spot relevant to its position in our solar system. They are all at their correct scale distance and of the correct size.

The centre of things – our sun – is to be found at Higher Lock, close to Newbury Farm Bridge number 24 and 400m along the towing path: in the other direction. On this scale, Pluto, almost too small to model is still 11km away. Similarly, on this scale, the average adult walking stride equals 400,000km.

To conceive the distances involved in space is almost impossible. But, graphically illustrated here is the fact that, to include the nearest star, there would need to be another 75,000 km of canal!

All the figures associated with this area are mind-blowing. The sun – our star – is a type G star of a size and type common in the universe. It's estimated to be about 5 billion years old with a similar time left, thus could it be said to be about mid-life (hope it doesn't have a mid life crisis). It is 149m km from earth and has a surface temperature of some 6,000°C. The sun is just one of an estimated 100 billion (100,000,000,000) stars in our galaxy (who counted them?), the Milky Way. That galaxy is just one of another 100 billion in the universe. The nearest star is *Proxima Centauri*, which is 4.3 light years away – 41 million km. The whole concept is a wonderful way of putting this business into perspective: but how do you imagine 100 billion would look?

The Somerset Space Walk was opened by Heather Couper at an event hosted by British Waterways – owners of the canal – on August 9th 1997.

Continue along the towing path to Coxhill Bridge (number 26) and leave up a ramp, through a kissing-gate to the road and turn right. Take the first turn to the right, which goes up what appears to be a farm drive. There is no footpath sign, the only marking being to Eames Farm.

The drive runs parallel to the road for a short time and then swings round to the right. About 200m down the driveway on the left in the wire fencing is a stile-like construction. Cross this (a footpath sign is now located here) and straight across the field. On the opposite side, another stile exits the field, leading into the farm track at the other side.

Walk straight ahead. At the top, is a junction with your road, which goes very slightly left, then right, and then more or less straight on, passing a cottage which sports a small moat. Ignore the road to the left. At the next junction, Prideaux House is on the right. Keep close to this, ignoring two more left turns.

The lane swings gently right around this house and then swings left again. As it does so, a grass track leads to the right to another group of buildings. Again, there is no signpost to guide you. Then, go over a stile and into a metalled lane amid a group of houses. Here, turn

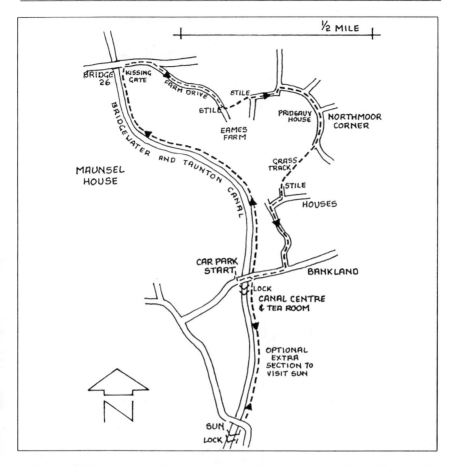

right, walking along what appears to be a private drive but is the right of way. The track then reaches what appears to be a T-junction; turn right. Follow the little lane as it twists and turns.

Go past a place called 'Herons Mead' and a very attractive thatched pink cottage with an equally attractive garden. At the next T-junction, turn right – another completely unmarked turning – and follow this road which leads back to the canal. Turn left by the bridge for the tea room.

Having arrived at the tea room, do consider a stroll in the opposite direction along the towing path towards Higher Lock. As mentioned, it is not far to walk and will help to bring some meaning to this space thing.

---

13. Burnham-on-Sea

Distance:	7½ or 8¼ miles.
Start:	The Tiny Tea Parlour, The Esplanade, Burnham-on-Sea.
Grid reference:	ST 303493
Parking:	On-street in the vicinity.

To the coast now and Burnham-on-Sea. This is a small but popular resort with long expanses of sandy beaches and dunes, particularly to the north. There is also a links golf course in this area, a real challenge to those who play this game.

The Tea Shop

The Tiny Tea Parlour is a place of real character. They have chairs upstairs that came from a church, witnessed by a hymn book rack in the back. There is a glorious display of old teapots between the ground and first floor and the walls are loaded with ephemera, mainly of a nautical or fishing flavour. The food is adequate in both quantity and quality with anything from a sandwich to a full three-course meal available. Do try a knickerbocker glory; they are magnificent.

The Tiny Tea Parlour opens at 12 noon every day. There are tables outside on the Esplanade overlooking the sea and giving a slightly continental feel, but traffic whizzing past destroys that illusion quite quickly. From the first floor, views over the bay are extensive and the front window seat has a pair of binoculars (chained down in case you have any naughty thoughts) with which to watch shipping in the Bristol Channel.

The parish church of St Andrews is probably the most interesting building in town. Parts of it date from 1316, but the piece which probably gives it the most character is the tower. This is the work of Sir Christopher Wren (1632-1723). Intriguingly, it has now acquired a decided list to starboard. This is due to the inability of the sandy foundations to support the weight. It is safe though and although it leans over Pisa-like, there is no danger of the collapse threatening that Italian masterpiece.

But the real treasure is inside. James II commissioned a marble altar reredos from Inigo Jones (1573-1652). The work was executed by Grinling Gibbons (1648-1721), the Dutch-born Englishman. The work was for the chapel of Whitehall Palace. It was rescued from there when fire struck and ended in Westminster Abbey via Hampton Court.

George IV disposed of it in 1820 and it was rescued by Bishop King of Rochester who was also vicar of Burnham. Thus the fragmented remains ended up here. Do make an effort to see them – they are sublime.

The Walk

In Burnham, turn right outside the tea shop and right into Adam Street. Walk straight across at the next crossroads and at the far end, turn right into Oxford Street followed immediately by a left into Jaycroft Road. Walk down this road to the far end. Here, directly ahead is a house and to the right of it, a narrow passage. Walk along here, bear right at the end and after only a few yards, left into a tree-lined close of relatively new housing. Although not noted at the bottom, this will eventually reveal itself as Quantock Close. Walk to the end of here and along Rosewood Close to a main road; turn right.

Continue along this road to a traffic island and go straight on ahead. Slightly to the left is the target for today: Brent Knoll. Beyond this island, after 100m there is a track down to a wooden fence beside a tree. Cross this fence in the obvious place and into a field, bearing right to walk alongside a watercourse. Continue through an open gateway – still quite close to the road – with a tall post indicating the footpath back to Burnham-on-Sea.

Cross this field, aiming for a small gap in the hedge opposite where a small bridge made of old railway sleepers is crossed. Here, turn half left towards a gate. Cross this, over a watercourse and walk alongside the left of this water, heading for a barrier guarding the railway line. Climb a stile to cross the line – care needed, high-speed track – and across a stile at the far side. Turn left here, between the railway and a caravan park. After some 150m, a right turn through a gate gives access to the caravan park; this is the route of the walk.

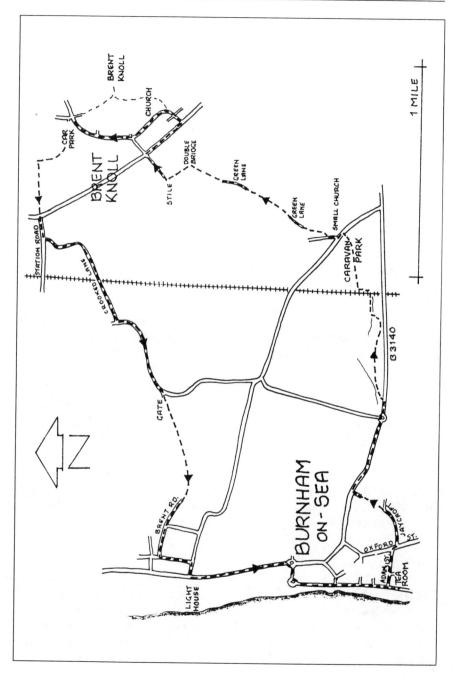

It is a splendid site, with all sorts of activities and refreshments, including cream tea. There is also a shop available.

Exit through their main gates and turn left, followed by the first right after a few metres.

There is a delightfully quaint church on the corner, a tiny corrugated iron construction, part of the Parish of St Andrews Burnham-on-Sea, Edithmead.

The church at Edithmead

Continue up the lane for some 150m. On the right-hand side, well buried in trees is a path between two flourishing hedges; a finger post marks the way. Walk down this narrow, tree-lined path, over another sleeper footbridge and, with the hedge to your left shoulder, aim slightly to the left of the church on the hill. Follow the hedge round this field until you reach a gate in the top corner, ignoring a previous gate and another sleeper bridge.

This gate leads into a green lane. Follow this to the top and take the entrance into the left-hand field and walk diagonally left across yet another sleeper bridge over a ditch. Cross this field to a gate, which leads to another green lane. At the top of here, walk straight ahead across the field, keeping the hedge to the left shoulder.

At the end, a variation. This is a double sleeper bridge alongside an older single one. Cross this, and turn left, heading alongside the watercourse to a stile in the far corner. Cross this and turn immediately right. This delivers the walk into yet another green lane, which eventually reaches a road passing an ancient walled garden *en route*. Turn right, down the village street.

> The village of Brent Knoll is also known as South Brent, to identify it from the hill. It is a long straggly affair, lining each side of the road but with precious little depth. There are few buildings of real interest, the oldest being Briers Cottage, which dates back to 1688.

Take the first on the left which is Church Lane. As the road climbs steeply and swings sharply to the left in front of the church, a public footpath signposted 'The Knoll', leaves to the right through a gate in some metal railings. Here, there is the opportunity to shorten the walk a little. Turn left and follow the road past St Michael's church.

> The church of St Michael is worth a visit. It is of Norman origin, the doorway from that time still extant. Inside, there are some quite remarkable carvings on the bench ends. Local legend has it that, many centuries ago, the local vicar was in conflict with the abbot of Glastonbury who was demanding local tithes be paid to him. The vicar resisted, and won.
>
> This event was celebrated in the carvings. There is a fox, dressed in abbot's attire rounding up some farmyard animals. Then the 'fox' is in the stocks and finally, depicted being hung: with geese pulling the rope. The monks' heads are also shown as pigs. It's a lovely legend but whether or not it is true is open to debate. But, as one learned newspaper editor wrote many years ago. "When truth and legend collide, print the legend".

Continue to a junction and turn right. Walk up the hill to a car parking area and turn left along a footpath. ***The main walk rejoins at this point.***

For the full walk, follow the track to the top and pause, take a breather after the effort and admire the superb views in every direction: if the weather is clear.

> The hill we know as Brent Knoll has a history as long as your arm. The

137m peak (450ft) has evidence of settlement during the Iron Age and a fort there is believed to have been some 1.6ha (4 acres) in area. The views enjoyed then would have been completely different from what we experience today. As mentioned elsewhere, much of this area was water or marsh for most of the year.

The fort was reinstated at the time of the Danish invasions of the ninth century. A collection of men from Dorset fought a battle on the slopes in 856 but the exact location is not clearly recorded. However, it is entirely reasonable to associate Battlebridge Farm on the southern slope – which was already established as a farm by that date – as the site.

Then, take the track down the other side until the walk reaches a road.

Whether or not you have been up the hill, cross the road and continue along a footpath through the courtesy car park following the clearly defined path. As the parking field widens out, turn half-right and then pause to admire the views over the Mendips. Even for those having taken the shorter route, this point is still on a high ridge giving the chance to admire similar views. In the opposite top corner of the field between a gate and the hedge of a garden is a stile. Cross this and walk around the left-hand edge of the field. Halfway around, there is a small opening that drops steeply down to another stile which leads very steeply down the hill: care is needed here. This leads down to a road.

Opposite is Station Road. Walk down here for 150m and turn left into an tiny road – Crooked Lane – which makes a series of bends and crosses the railway line before reaching a somewhat rudimentary T-junction. Bear left here and at the end, only 100m along, is a much lesser path to the left; the walk follows the bridleway to the right. Some 800m along, the main bridleway bears left. Ahead is a gate with a pedestrian gate alongside which is the walk.

This track develops into a road – eventually identified as Brent Road – which reaches a T-junction where a left turn into Brambles Road is made. At the end of here, turn right, then left at the main road, close to the site of an old lighthouse – now converted to domestic use. Follow this to a traffic island, turn right to reach the sea front and left, back to the tea room.

```
┌─────────────────────────────────────────────────────────┐
│                                                         │
│                    14. Taunton                          │
│                                                         │
└─────────────────────────────────────────────────────────┘
```

Distance: 2 miles.
Start: The riverside car park at Priory Bridge Road, Taunton.
Grid reference: ST 227252
Parking: At the start.

The county town of Somerset, Taunton is a delightful place with much to attract the visitor: and walker.

This town has seen some tumultuous times over the centuries. Records of a Saxon castle around 710 exist and that same site was where the Normans built their fortifications. Part of that work – the keep – still remains with its 4m thick wall.

Taunton has also seen its share of intrigue over the centuries. It was a Parliamentarian stronghold during the Civil War and was placed under – and withstood – a siege. It was here in 1497, that Perkin Warbeck, a Flemish impostor, was proclaimed King of England. He claimed to be Richard Duke of York who had earlier been murdered in the Tower of London. Gaining some credence and limited support in Ireland, France and Scotland, Warbeck landed in the west country and laid siege to Exeter for a while before arriving in Taunton. Henry VII was hot on his trail as Perkin headed for Beaulieu in Hampshire. He was arrested there, removed to the Tower and executed.

Taunton was also where James Scott, the Duke of Monmouth was proclaimed King James II in June 1685. He was an illegitimate offspring of Charles II, one of thirteen sired by this randy royal who certainly earned the sobriquet of 'The Merry Monarch'.

James Scott had been in exile since 1683 after taking part in the Rye House Plot to kill Charles II and his brother James. James had converted to Catholicism in 1668 and was deeply unpopular when he ascended the throne in February 1685 as the legitimate James II. Nationally, there were real fears of a Catholic tyranny after his accession. Taking advantage of this, Monmouth landed at Lyme Regis in Dorset with a hundred or so followers. Heading west, he recruited a rag-tag force of some 2,500 miners and agricultural workers and 600 horse soldiers.

After the Proclamation, he set out on July 6th 1685, with his army towards Sedgemoor in an attempt to surprise the King's troops who had headed west to deal with this uprising. The only surprise was the strength of the king's artillery who decimated Monmouth's forces as they tried to cross a drainage ditch. Monmouth fled, was arrested, taken to the Tower of London where he was beheaded on July 15th. The wheels of justice moved exceedingly fast in those days.

This was the last battle ever fought on English soil. It also resulted in the name of George Jeffreys becoming even more infamous. A willing tool of King James, he rose to prominence at the trial of Titus Oates and was sent west to try those involved in this uprising. The Bloody Assizes were the result with hundreds executed or transported. These were held in the Great Hall of the Castle.

The Castle today houses the Somerset County Museum and is well worth a visit. Many fascinating aspects of local history are on display, some mentioned on other pages within this book. It also tells the story of the Somerset Light Infantry on their campaigns around the world.

Riverside, Taunton

The Tea Shops

Overture's restaurant and bar. This is open all day for tea and coffee, and has a selection of home-made cake, biscuits and lunches with plenty of vegetarian options. There are benches set out very close to the river giving you the outdoor option on a nice day. It is also a craft shop and gallery.

The **Riverside Coffee Lounge** has a good menu with substantial meals at lunch and a splendid afternoon tea. The place is clean and bright with modern furnishings including Formica tables and chromium plated chairs. An upstairs room looks out over the river Tone.

The Walk

Leave the car park by walking to the river's edge and turning left. Head off down beside the water passing – but not crossing – a new bridge with round concrete pillars and red painted ironwork. To match, the nice new path then becomes a tree lined avenue as young trees, growing between the path and the river push their branches ever further towards the Somerset sky; thoroughly pleasant.

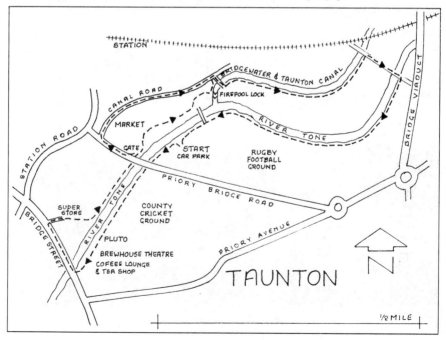

On the left is the back of Somerset County Cricket Club ground. For many years a relative backwater of the county game, Somerset finally began to make an impression on the county game about the same time as a sublimely talented young man started thrashing a ball about this ground. His name? Ian Botham. Yes, this is where his natural skills were honed under the watchful eye of ex-Yorkshire captain, Brian Close. The rest, as they say, is history.

Subsequently, other immortals of the cricketing world have graced the club. Perhaps the most gifted was former West Indies skipper, Viv Richards.

Within the ground is the Somerset Cricket Museum. A huge collection of cricketing memorabilia is on display and there is an extensive reference library of immense value to scholars of this wonderful game.

Continue along the river bank to a car park and rudimentary gardens.

Here, there is a good view of the towers of St Mary Magdalene church. There is a stone set up at the far end of this car park representing the planet of Pluto. The reason for this strange edifice is revealed during Walk 12.

Pass the rear of the Brewhouse theatre.

We are now in the area of tea-shops. Immediately beside the theatre is Overture's restaurant and bar. And, staying beside the river, just before the ornate turquoise and white bridge you have the Riverside Coffee Lounge.

Continue to the bridge. Here, leave the path, walk up to the bridge and turn right to cross it. At the far side, turn right again into Woodlands Lane which leads down past Safeways and back to the river.

Again, if you feel like it, you could stop in Safeways and have another meal as they have an attractive café with big circular windows. The menu was somewhat restricted on my visit, comparing badly with the fare on offer across the water. Perhaps I caught them on a bad day.

Continue the walk alongside the river, walking back the way you came but on the opposite bank, through attractive looking gardens with seats and under the main road bridge.

There is a choice of routes here. Ahead, the path arrives at a gate into Taunton Cattle Market. When this is not operational, you can walk right through. If you need to divert, pick up the instructions at **ALTERNATIVE ROUTE.**

Keep the river on your right, walk straight through the market and out the far side until the perimeter fence turns left, indicating the end of the surfaced area. Ahead, the river. Turn left and follow the fence for another 50m and, on the right, the car park extends to the right again. Here, just around the corner is a wooden gate, which gives access to Firepool Lock. Walk a few yards towards the other end of the lock and on the left is a path, which leads away from the water's edge to a lane. Turn right.

ALTERNATIVE ROUTE: Leave the river here and walk up to Priory Bridge Road. Cross and turn left, taking the first right into Canal Road. This reaches a bridge across the canal where the two options rejoin.

> This is where the Bridgwater and Taunton Canal left the river Tone on its way to Bridgwater. For a more detailed look at this canal, see Walk 12. Also in this area, the Grand Western Canal arrived from Tiverton. More details of this unusual canal can also be discovered in Walk 12.

Cross the bridge and bear left, following the towpath alongside the canal. This is good firm walking. Continue along here to the first road bridge, leave the canal, walk up the ramp to the road and turn right. This is a cycleway, as the arrows indicate.

Continue along the road to the next bridge and turn right, still along the cycleway – watch out for high-speed cyclists. Walk down to – and alongside – the river along a quality paved path back to the car park.

> As all the paths on this short walk are in good condition, it is very much a clean shoe affair, not requiring sturdy walking boots.

15. Nether Stowey

Distance:	1½ miles.
Start:	Stowey Tea Rooms, Castle Street, Nether Stowey.
Grid reference:	ST 191397
Parking:	Off-road car park in Castle Street.

Nether Stowey is an archetypal English village. There is a central road through the place, the remains of a castle, thatched cottages, a stream through the main street and literary history. Add in a tea room of character and all the ingredients are in place. The whole village is a Conservation Area.

The only thing absent which is missed not at all, is a main road. The A39 Minehead to Taunton road once came through here but the place seized solid during the summer months and a by-pass was constructed as early as 1969; which probably gives a good indication of how urgently it was needed.

The Tea Shops

The selected establishment in Nether Stowey is a real tea shop with a fine range of teas including Darjeerling, Earl Grey, Assam or Fruit. Then there is hot chocolate and coffee. Cream teas and toasted sandwiches and a range of other light snacks complete the menu.

Should this establishment be closed, a few metres down the road – on the same side – is **Castle Cottage**. Three hundred years old with head banging low beams, it is an equal attraction.

The Walk

Turn left from the car park and walk down Castle Street, past the tea room. At the bottom, turn left.

> Another aspect of an English village is the stream running through the centre of Nether Stowey. With tiny bridges to allow access to each property, it adds a delightful atmosphere to the place.

Walk along Lime Street for around 200m and on the left is Coleridge Cottage.

It is perhaps possible that a visit to Nether Stowey will inspire you as it inspired the great poet, Samuel Taylor Coleridge. He moved there, aged twenty-five, in 1797, and lived there for three years with his young wife, Sara. His communist ideas were still fomenting at this time. He met William and Dorothy Wordsworth who then lived in nearby Holford (see Walk 17). The two poets walked the Quantocks together, each gaining inspiration for their work. With some input from Wordsworth, Coleridge wrote 'The Rime of the Ancient Mariner' at that time.

His ability of self-parody is clear from another poem entitled: 'To The Author of the Ancient Mariner'.

> *Your poem must eternal be,*
> *Dear Sir! it cannot fail!*
> *For 'tis incomprehensible,*
> *And without a head or tail.*

And although his 'Kubla Khan' was not published until 1816, it is believed to have been the result of his days in this house.

> *In Xanadu did Kubla Khan*
> *A stately pleasure dome decree:*
> *Where Alph, the sacred river, ran*
> *Through caverns measureless to man*
> *Down to a sunless sea.*

The house is under the care of the National Trust and is open April to September, Tuesday to Thursday and Sundays, 2pm to 5pm, telephone 01278 732662.

You don't need a second guess at the name of the pub across the road. But The Ancient Mariner is good for all that: food and fine, real Midlands ales.

Continue along Lime Street. Just past the Coleridge house, the footpath goes away to the left up to the top of a bank concealed from but alongside the road. This turns left into Mill Lane and ends. Walk down a grassy bank, cross Coleridge Road up the bank at the other side and continue along another concealed path. This ends after 100m and the roadside is then used. Walk past a sign 'Audley Close' and 25m along take the next left into a narrow lane. A further 25m along here, on the right are two public footpaths. Take the second one with a fingerpost indicating the way to Stowey Castle, up the hill.

This leads over the mound that was once Stowey Castle with its commanding views of the surrounding countryside and beyond, to a stile. Cross this and walk down to the road. Directly opposite, across the road, follow another footpath, which takes the walk ahead for a few metres before turning left and dropping down over the hill.

This leads to a well used pathway fenced one side and hedged the other, through a kissing-gate and onto a road opposite **The Arches and The Gables**. Turn right, down this road and continue until it starts to swing round to the right. As it does so, turn off to the left down Baneson Road. This sweeps gently to the right and then left, followed by another right, just before it ends. Here, turn left, down the well-surfaced track. At the end, opposite St Mary's Church Centre, you turn left into the village and left again into Castle Street.

If you have not yet satisfied your urge for cheese, there is another fine establishment a few metres to the right. At this point, over across the main road is Cricket Malherbie Creamery. This company was established by the late Lord Beaverbrook – the famous newspaper proprietor and minister of Supply in Churchill's wartime cabinet in 1948 and purchased by its present owners, the Jeanes family in 1978. They had been cheese-

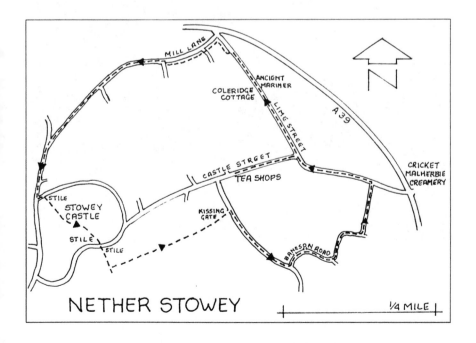

NETHER STOWEY

makers in the area for decades before that same war brought production to an end, never to re-start.

What they did then was to concentrate on milk production, actually supplying this creamery with its raw material. Having joyfully returned to the cheese-making fold, the Jeanes set about their business with gusto. Realising that tourists drove past their door every day, they have provided a viewing area so you can watch their craftsmen engaged in the manufacturing process. In the room, a video explains what's happening.

Then on to the shop. Small samples allow you to taste what is available. One taste, and you're sure to buy: it's not overly expensive either. There are a variety of other dairy products on sale, both made in-house and bought in, together with other Epicurean delights. And, to prove your ineffable good taste, the shop and dairy are festooned with rosettes and certificates won at shows around the country.

Strange ornamentation in a garden at Nether Stowey

16. Handy Cross

Distance:	3½ miles.
Start:	Handy Cross Farmhouse, Lydeard St Lawrence.
Grid reference:	ST 123316
Parking:	Outside the tea room.

This area is rural Somerset at its best. Gone are the Levels; the Quantocks rear away to the east and up hill and down dale will describe this area. But do not worry, none of the hills are steep and there is a visit to an attractive manor house *en route*. Note also that we are back into the area of small fields, hedgerows with wild flowers and birds, and flocks of sheep. There are no arable prairies in this corner of Somerset.

The farmhouse tea-room at Handy Cross

The Tea Shop

The tea room is a pretty little affair, located in an ancient farmhouse. A fifteenth century entrance hall leads into an eighteenth century room, which is where the food is served. An excellent choice is on offer, from straightforward teas through to quiche, ploughman's lunch, and an assortment of other lunches. Behind, the owners have opened a Collectors Centre. This is essentially a bric-a-brac shop but with a pretty good range of antiques as well.

The Walk

Leave the tea room turning left and walk along the road, taking a right at the cross-roads. 250m along on the right is the drive to a bungalow. Immediately to the left of this drive is a stile. Cross this into a field. Follow roughly the line of the electricity poles towards some trees. At the far end of the field, the path passes a gate and runs alongside woodlands.

Keep the hedge to the wood on your right shoulder. After the third gateway, the ground drops away to your left towards a little valley, opening out some quite attractive views. As you round the next corner, still keeping the hedge to your right, is a tower, directly ahead on the skyline.

As the tree line takes a sharp turn to the right, you head away up the opposite hill across the fields. Aim to carry on in a straight line, slightly to the right of the top of the hill where there is an opening in the fence, which drops you into the fields just to the right-hand side of the farm. Head straight down out of the trees, cross the farm track at the bottom over to the far side, where a gate drops you into another green lane. Turn left down the farm track back onto the road, and then turn right and walk down the road.

Next, turn left at the first junction and then, after 200m – immediately behind the village sign for Tolland – a bridleway goes off to the left. This climbs a short way between some trees out into a field and then drops very slightly to the right. It then carries on along slightly above, but parallel, to the stream. It's quite a clearly marked path to start with. Walk between the gorse bushes and head towards the kissing-gate ahead. The stream down to the right is full of watercress. What a shame that the risk of liver fluke makes this dangerous to pick.

Through the gate, (which does not close very easily), the path goes back into a wooded area. Drop down until you are tight against the stream by a tiny waterfall. Here, the path turns slightly to the left.

If you are lucky and can walk quietly, you may surprise a heron fishing in the stream. This really is quite a beautiful area with very fine tall straight ash trees. There are also sycamore, oak and beech growing. In the autumn this is quite a 'collect and gather' walk. Be prepared to take time out to gather blackberries, beech nuts and even field mushrooms. On both sides of the path, it is possible to see badger setts and the numerous tracks hereabouts are certainly down to these delightful creatures.

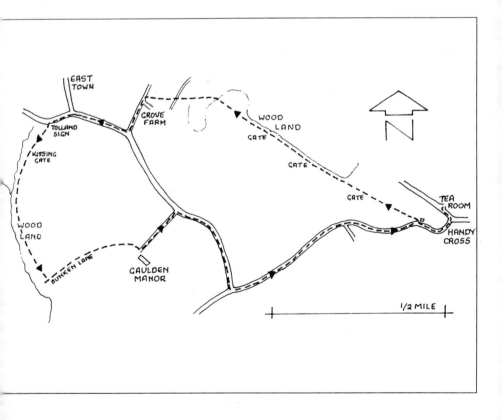

The walk then drops down a little to meet a T-junction. Turn left, slightly uphill on a well-used west country style sunken lane. Your path then leads to a road. This is the drive to Gaulden Manor, which stands directly ahead. If you are visiting the Manor, walk across to the entrance, if not, turn left.

> Privately owned but open to visitors, Gaulden Manor has parts that were originally built in the twelfth century. Constructed from the local pink sandstone, the main house has delightfully decorated plasterwork, which dates back to the early 1600s. This was carried out by John Turberville. His family owned the manor until 1699 and were descendants of the ones made famous by the writer Thomas Hardy.
>
> The garden here is of great interest. Twenty years ago it was a wilderness, but a concerted effort by the owners has seen it turned into an absorbing experience. Divided into small areas, the 'Little Gardens of Gaulden' offer roses, herbs, butterflies and a bog garden.

Return to the drive and walk up to the road. Turn right here and follow this lane to a T-junction. Turn left and walk along the road, past the bungalow on the left where the walk set off across field and back to the main road. Turn left, back to the tea room.

17. Holford

Distance:	4½ miles.
Start:	Holford village, west of the A39 Minehead to Taunton road.
Grid reference:	ST 15411
Parking:	Car park by the bowling green.

There is no grandiose scenery to be discovered on this walk, no ancient ruins; in fact, nothing much at all. But, having walked it, the route is one of the most satisfying in this book. Almost entirely away from civilisation, the routes are used but little and the chance of walking for hours without seeing another soul is great.

So beautiful is this area that one of England's foremost poets was inspired to describe its beauty in verse: as we will see later. There is woodland, open hillsides with views out into the Bristol Channel and the incomparable Quantocks, smallest yet arguably one of the prettiest ranges of hills in this country. That was recognised over forty years ago when they were established as England's first Area of Outstanding Natural Beauty. It is a nature-lover's paradise. In the deep woods, dormice and badgers flourish and out amongst the bracken; rare flowers and hosts of insects. Overhead, you will see a huge range of butterflies, moths and birds.

There are only thirty-six square miles to the Quantock and the peaks themselves are only minor hills. The second tallest, Robin Upright's Hill, is at the northern end of the range, close to this walk. It stands 357m (1,170ft) high.

On top of some of these hills can be found evidence of prehistoric man having lived here. Round burial mounds (barrows) from the Bronze Age can be found, as can Iron Age hill forts. One of these sits atop Downsborough, the large hill at the head of Holford Combe.

The Tea Shop

Although actually a small hotel, the **Combe House Hotel** fits our purposes as a tea room admirably. It is a seventeenth century building offering a delightfully traditional version of afternoon tea in the most elegant of surrounds. Sadly, there are no other tea rooms actually up in the hills, so this stroll into the northern reaches must suffice.

The Walk

From the car park alongside the Quantock Hill Holford Bowling Green, turn right, heading back into the village. Turn right – as the road swings sharp left – opposite a delightful row of thatched cottages. Walk along this lane, bearing to the left, which takes you past the right-hand edge of the cottages. At the next road, turn right. This is signposted, Holford Combe – No Through Road. Walking along this road, which is starting to climb gently, the **Coombe House Hotel** will be found on the right-hand side.

> The building itself has been upgraded and modernised over the years without destroying the traditional aspect of it. To the left-hand side of the main building is a water wheel, reputed to be the third largest in the country. Its millstream still flows through the five acres of delightfully lawned grounds where the huge monkey puzzle tree stands, close to a gnarled and ancient yew.

Leave the hotel, turn right and walk up the lane, a tree-covered affair that almost creates a tunnel. This is well used; for the moment. On the right is a hedge enclosing a small field. Beyond, a noisy stream with waterfalls hurries down towards the Bristol Channel. This leads into a delightful open area close to the stream.

In this clearing, turn right and walk through the shallow water to a track up the opposite hill. There is no bridge, so some form of waterproof footwear is essential. The clearly defined path heads gently uphill through the trees between two small hills and up a narrow valley.

As the edge of the woods is reached, the path forks; take the right-hand one, down over a tiny stream. This path becomes quite narrow as it clings to the side of a hill, circling round the hill to the right.

The path continues to climb – still between two hills – and eventually the walk circles right around the one to the left. Behind is a large, bare hill. The walk then leaves the trees and enters an area of bracken together with holly trees.

This path then reaches a T-junction; take the right-hand turn and almost immediately, the walk hacks off back, sharply to the left.

A pause here to admire the dramatic views over the Quantocks is almost obligatory.

At the next junction after 100m, keep right and as you reach the crest of the hill, carry straight on where this track crosses another tiny path. The walk then drops down over the other side of the hill towards a wooded valley directly ahead. Underfoot, the grass soon

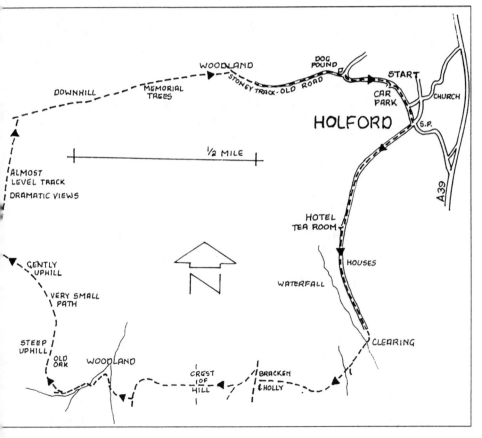

changes to stone as more holly trees appear and the path descends quite steeply towards deciduous woodland and the stream. Some 100m from the stream, a fork in the path appears; take the one that turns steeply right, down towards the stream into an enchanting area of woodland by the stream.

Cross the water (no bridge again) and turn half right away from the water heading just around the base of a little hillock to the left. This leads into a little valley where the other half of this stream is running. On reaching the next stream, a very clear path runs alongside. Turn left, heading gently upstream – albeit not tight to the water; perhaps 20m away. The path then curves and crosses the stream, continuing up on the opposite (right-hand) side of the water. This is a broad stone track through oak woodland with a tiny stream on the left.

Take the first turn to the right, some 300m along, which sets off gently up the side of a hill, climbing and circling to the right around the hill, eventually climbing through a very small valley away from the stream.

> On the right here is an amazing old oak tree. It gives the impression of being coppiced at some time. The gnarled old trunk stands some 2m tall. From this, dozens of branches have sprung out in all directions creating an extraordinary effect.
>
> Quantock oaks were a favoured crop in years gone by. Not only were they used for making charcoal but the tanning industry also demanded a regular supply.

The path then starts to narrow, eventually becoming little more than a tiny sheep track. Carry on, up the hill aiming to cross the top. On reaching higher ground, the views start to unfold dramatically. Over to the right, Nether Stowey, (visited in Walk 15) and the flat Somerset Levels.

This track eventually swings around to the left as it continues steadily uphill: high, but not steep. A clearly defined track then crosses the walk route, close to the crest of the hill. Turn right, heading towards the Somerset Levels.

> Brent Knoll (Walk 13) is clearly visible from here on the right, the Bristol Channel directly ahead. Beyond there, is the coast of South Wales.

After some 300m, the path splits; take the right-hand one which is pretty well straight ahead. Cross the hill with Hinckley Point nuclear power station directly ahead in the distance. This track then meets a very well-used (and worn) track running diagonally across. Join it, turning half right heading down the hill towards a clump of firs.

> Below the circle of trees is a memorial stone explaining that these trees were planted in memory of the men and women who fought during the last war from Holford and Kilve (another small community almost two miles north of this spot).

Carry on down over the hill into the wood. Here, a very rough stone track is encountered, running diagonally across. Turn right heading down to the right-hand side. This runs through an area of trees, obviously a well-used track. There are a lot of sweet chestnuts growing in this area. This brings the walk down to a road on the point of a hairpin bend.

> On this junction to the left is a somewhat decrepit ruin. It is actually an ancient dog pound. These remains were given to the village of Holford in 1982, by the family of the late John Lancelot Brereton, who were descendants of the St Albyns, owners of Alfoxton since the fifteenth century. The family crest is displayed on a plaque on the wall.
>
> To the left, up the hill, is Alfoxton House. Today, it is a hotel, but in 1797, William Wordsworth rented it. Together with his sister Dorothy, he ranged far and wide around the Quantocks. At this time, Samuel Taylor Coleridge

lived in Nether Stowey, (see Walk 15) and they spent many hours together. Although normally associated with the Lake District, Wordsworth was at his most inspired whilst living in Somerset. His *Lyrical Ballads* (1798), published with Coleridge, is generally thought to best display his creativity. Indeed, this almost seminal work, marked the movement away from the neo-classic artificiality then ruling. Coleridge's 'Rime of the Ancient Mariner' opened this book and Wordsworth's 'Tintern Abbey' was the last one.

The lines from 'Upon Smooth Quantock's airy ridge we roved' referred to the head of the Holford Combe, the area through which this walk has passed.

Walk straight ahead and follow the road back into Holford where the car park will be discovered on the right-hand side.

18. Washford

Distance:	3 miles.
Start:	Torre Valley Cider Farm, Hungerford, Washford.
Grid reference:	ST 047401
Parking:	At the tea room.

On this walk, there is a real chance to sample the product everyone associates with the county of Somerset: cider.

There are several cider farms in this part of the country and this one is quite representative. There is ample scope to see the whole process: if you pick the right time of year. Obviously, autumn is the peak of activity as the new season's crop of apples is being delivered.

Torre Valley Cider farm is very much a cottage industry with no great orchards supplying tons of fruit. You are much more likely to see a local farmer roll up with a few boxes of fruit in the back of his Landrover.

Steve and Janet Gillman have spent over ten years building up this place. It is very much a traditional operation. The fruit is unloaded into a stockpile and a 'cheese' prepared. This is a layer of apples carefully laid out on cloth. Another layer of cloth and apple follows until a huge sandwich is created. This is the cheese. Then an hydraulic press is brought to bear and the juice squeezed out. In days of yore, this process was carried out by hand, a huge bar being used to force the press downwards.

To emphasise how traditional it is, the couple have a Gloucester Black Spot pig, wonderfully named Cynthia. She is responsible for eating the pulped remains of the fruit: and a very efficient job she does too.

The cider they manufacture is – of course – available for sale. But, a sincere word of warning. This stuff is wonderful – probably what angels drink at break time. But it does have a hidden message. Tasting astonishingly full of fruit, the alcohol content is not at all obvious. "Nothing to this stuff", you may well say to yourself as the second pint disappears down your neck. Giving the lie to this, your legs then chart their own particular loopy way, impervious to any commands from you. It is real 'falling down water', certainly not to be swilled on a hot day and empty stomach: unless you have a death wish. Taken in a sensible fashion, it is simply superb.

The Tea Shop

The tea room offers the usual range of goodies with nice tables and seats outside where you may enjoy them. They also sell honey, jams and chutney and have a small pick-your-own strawberry field. A splendid enterprise indeed.

The Walk

Leave the cider farm and turn left, up the road, taking the first left into a driveway. This leads to the gates of what appears to be a storage area for stone and sand where the footpath turns right in front of the gates. Quite clearly marked, this runs beside a chain link fence. Cross a stile and almost immediately there is a barrier with three bars. Over that, the path leads across a field.

Keep to the left of the hedge and pass through the gate in the top right-hand corner into a sunken green lane and continue straight ahead. Two huge pillars, made of small bits of stone – clearly gate posts at some time – stand at this point.

Carry on down the lane which is a completely rough track between two hedges. Approaching the buildings of a farm, there is a track that sweeps round to the left and into a field. Here is a 'Footpath to Washford' sign which indicates that the route is to the left, through a gate and across a field.

At the top of that field, take the left-hand gateway, keeping the hedge to the right. Cross this field and in the bottom right corner is a metal gate. Through here is a meeting of the ways. Three footpaths converge; the route of this walk is left, over a new stile. Cross this field keeping the hedge on the left this time as the field on the right rises to the crest of a small hill.

Over the stile at the end of that field, the walk reaches a small lane. Carry on straight ahead. To the right, immediately beyond the stile is a children's play area. As the road swings left, the walk follows a footpath that goes straight ahead through another scrubby, wooded area. Pass a row of garages to a metalled path which leads to a road. Walk straight ahead here to the main road.

Turn right, but please note; this is an extremely busy road with no footpath and extreme care must be taken. Leave the road by turning left after some 200m and follow this road over a bridge across a stream and into the village of Washford, all pretty cottages and thatched roofs, and the village school on the left.

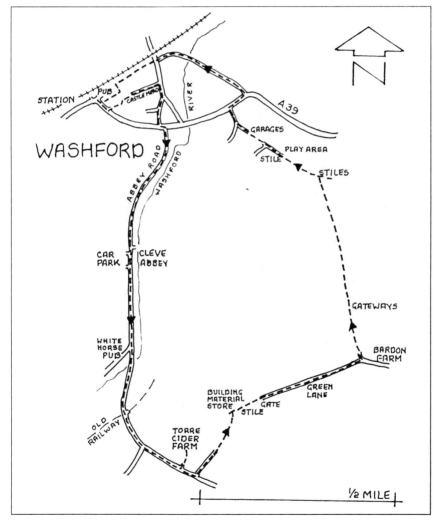

At the next T-junction, directly ahead is a path, alongside a railway bridge. Follow this. It will eventually turn sharp left and away from the railway for some 30m before turning right along a small alley, back on the original course but 30m away from the railway.

This path soon arrives at **The Washford Arms** and railway station. Should you eschew the delights here, turn left, back down the footpath alongside the main road.

> The pub itself is a pleasant hostelry offering good ale and fine food: and a view of steam trains as they rumble past the garden. Yes, steam. This is the West Somerset Railway.
>
> It was back on January 2nd 1971 that British Rail closed the line to passenger services. Apparently, there was not enough money to be made to satisfy their accountants. It was one of many closures around that era. The Beeching cuts of the mid-1960s had brought howls of protest in many quarters and some places had seen a change of heart. Condemned services were reprieved and supposed cost savings introduced.
>
> It was remarkable how many lines lasted around five years after the original storm; the loudest protesters had already discharged their large cannon after the initial proposals and most went quietly in the second wave.
>
> Fortunately, that was not the end of this particular story. Immediately after BR closed the line, a private company was formed to re-open it. They succeeded, bringing sections of track into use, offering their first service at Easter 1976.
>
> Since then, work has continued and now the whole length between Minehead and Bishops Lydeard reverberates to the sound of steam. The West Somerset is one of our foremost preserved lines with vintage steam and carriages mixed with discards from the more modern age of diesels.
>
> The original line used to run to Taunton but today it finishes a few miles short. This is because to get to Taunton station the new company would have to use the main line and you can't run preserved steam trains on high speed Railtrack lines. Still, the whole thing does very nicely thank you.

Walking back down the main road having turned left from the pub and railway, after 40m, take the path on the left, alongside a green. This delivers the walk into a road – Castle Mead – with housing on both sides. Continue to the end, turn right and take the first on the right, some 50m along. A sign indicates Claydon Close. Walk up here to the top of a rise and then straight ahead down the other side, past a large no entry sign and back to the main road. Turn left and cross the road almost immediately, turning right into Abbey Road. Walk up this road, alongside the stream, until you reach Cleeve Abbey on the left.

Cleeve Abbey

There are several unusual features to be enjoyed in the wonderful ruin, cared for by English Heritage. It was founded in the twelfth century by the Earl of Lincoln for an order of Cistercian monks. The drive passes through a gabled gatehouse, giving entry to a bewitching area of green with the remains somewhat at odds with the usual order of things.

At the Dissolution, the first buildings to be sacked were the living areas. The church or central areas of worship tended to be sacrosanct, often adopted for use by the fledging Church of England. Thus, we are well informed about the churches, less so about the associated buildings.

Cleeve sets that right. The cloister buildings are pretty well complete and the refectory has a magnificent wagon roof. There is a glorious rose window and exquisite vaulting.

Turn left as you leave the abbey and follow the road, keeping left past **The White Horse**.

This is another venerable building, part of which dates back to the thirteenth century. It was once used as a toll house and coaching inn.

Along this lane the remains of a railway level crossing will be discovered.

This is an ancient mineral railway that ran from the Brendon Hills to Watchet. Its purpose was to carry iron ore from quarries up there to the harbour where it was loaded aboard ships and sent to Ebbw Vale in South Wales. It has been closed now for a very long time but there is a small point of interest to seekers of railway archaeology. Some six miles to the south on a minor road at SS 023344, the railway crossed the road. To the north was an incline of 25 per cent (1:4) down which the loaded waggons of ore were despatched. It was almost a mile long and remains of this are still visible.

Continue along the road and back to the tea room.

19. Wimbleball Reservoir

Distance:	2½ or 4 miles.
Start:	Wimbleball Reservoir Information Centre.
Grid reference:	SS 965308
Parking:	At the Information Centre.

The South West Water reservoir at Wimbleball was completed in 1978 and holds 4,740 million gallons of water. It is one of only three that serves the whole of the west of England. Water from here is released into the river Exe. This river rises only a few miles from the north coast of Somerset but then runs generally south through Devon for fifty-five miles before emptying into the English Channel. The river is used as an open conduit to move water from here downstream to provide a service for Tiverton and, further along, Exeter.

It was formed by damming the river Haddeo, which rises on the side of the hill across the water. Several other minor streams origi-

Bird life at Wimbleball

nally ran through the valley. As an aside, the Haddeo then passes through a small wooded area known as Cuckold's Combe.

The Tea Shop

The tea and gift shop sells light refreshments, cream teas, ice cream and countryside gifts and is only open during the summer months. There are picnic tables around the area of the car park and the tea room offers an extremely pleasant view out over the reservoir.

The Walk

Leave the car park and head down towards the lake and past the play area. At the bottom turn right, through a gate, picking up a path which runs alongside but above the water. This path then circles round the back of the sailing club and through a kissing-gate where it turns left up a small flight of steps alongside the water. This section is known as the Upton Arm.

> How close the walk gets to the water's edge is dependent of the time of year. In summer, the water level tends to be well below, in winter, after a good rainfall, it gets quite close. There are regularly spaced seats to give the opportunity to pause and admire the scenery: and the activity. There is a whole range of birds and wildfowl that have colonised this man-made expanse of water. Canada geese in flocks are particularly noticeable. In season, the tiny sailing dinghies making their frenetic changes of direction can provide plenty of entertainment as well.

Pass the lower side of a farm and a wooden bridge over a dry dyke.

> Just over the bridge to the right are a wire fence and a gate. On that gate is the sign 'No Cars'. How you could possibly access the area by car is a complete mystery. The farm is Harewood Farm. Beyond, the land starts to slope much more steeply down to the reservoir and the path is higher up the side in a wooded area that is still benefiting from new planting. The Exmoor National Park takes in some of the most rugged scenery in this corner of England and its boundary runs along the top of Haddon Hill, which is the range of hills to the right.

Out of the trees, circle round to the right and come up to the dam. Here, there is a gate with a stile beside it. Cross and turn right. Walk

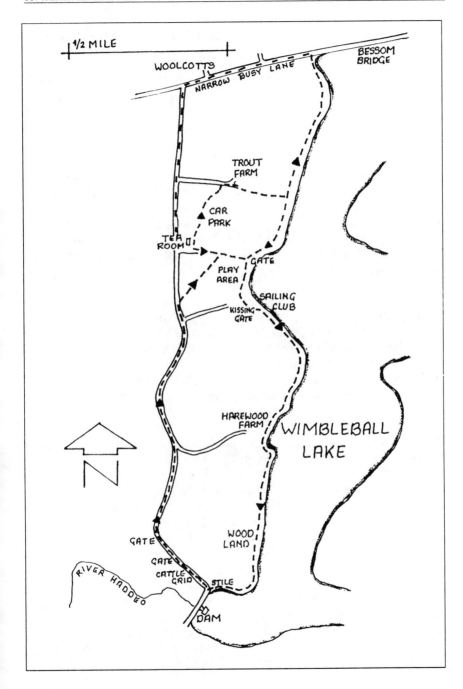

up the service road, away from the dam. Through a gate alongside a cattle grid.

Here, you can get a splendid view of the water over your shoulder with beautiful wooded Exmoor laid out all alongside the road. The views are not extensive because you are looking into the valleys but what can be seen is delightful, tranquil and quite remote.

The walk then passes through another kissing-gate beside a cattle grid and starts to climb up the hill. Then, another gate, and the climb is over. Continue along the track and walk straight ahead as it meets a road arriving uphill from the right. This finally reaches the entrance to the sailing club on the right. 20m along – also on the right – is a wooden gate and signpost. This leads back down to the water's edge, close to where the walk started. Turn left and retrace your steps to the car park.

Here, decision time, because the shorter walk ends here. To continue, pass the tea room and follow the path at the north end of the car park. This leads to a road; turn right, past Wimbleball Trout Fishery and continue along the path downhill to a crossroads. Turn left, above the small jetty where it is possible to hire fishing boats. Hugging the water, this path eventually leads to a road where Bessom Bridge crosses over a neck of the reservoir.

Four miles up this road to the right is Brendon Hill and the old mineral railway incline mentioned in Walk 18. There is also another picnic area just across the bridge and to the right.

There is a further extension to the walk if desired. Cross the road and take the track to the left into Hurscombe Plantation which is a nature reserve. This continues up the combe for 1.5 miles before reaching a road and a farm. Turn sharp right and follow another path due south for 1100m to a road. Turn right and the road leads back to Bessom Bridge.

Here, there is a choice. If you wish to avoid back-tracking, turn left, and first left again along the approach road to the car park. However, with the volume of traffic in this narrow lane, the favoured option by far is to return alongside the water to the gate encountered at the start of the walk and turn right, back to the car park.

20. Dunster

Distance:	5 miles.
Start:	Car park alongside the A396, between the A39 and the village.
Grid reference:	SS 993439
Parking:	Main park on edge of village, some street parking in centre.

Good things come in small packages. That proverb was never better illustrated than here in Dunster. Just after you leave the car park there is The Dunster Visitors Centre. Do call in. There is so much to discover about the place and surrounding countryside that time in there is time well spent.

As you walk through the centre of the village, the sheer beauty of the buildings will grab you. Lots of splendid shops line this wide main street, many of them tea rooms. In the square is the yarn market

The Yarn market in Dunster

which dates back to the 1580s when cloth was an important trade around here. The famed soft cloth known as Dunster is named after the village where it was made and sold.

The Tea Shops

Stand by the octagonal building and look around you. **The Willows Tea Rooms**, **Stables Restaurant**, **The Old House Garden Café** and **Castle Coffee House** are just a few of the refreshment houses in this hugely popular village. For that reason, on this walk alone, there is no recommended starting refreshment point.

The Walk

Leave the car park and turn left towards the village centre. As the road turns sharp left, take the road straight ahead, up a slight rise.

> On the left, on the bend is The Luttrell Arms. This dates back to the fifteenth century and, in those days, was the residence of the Abbots of Cleeve whose abbey we visit in Walk 18. The porch has loopholes for the use of archers.

This is The Ball. As it turns left, the road then becomes Priory Green. Walk along here to the Dovecote.

> The breeding of pigeons for food was a concept that came over with the Normans. Pigeon lofts or dovecotes were once known as *columbaria*, a term that came from the Romans. In the seventeenth century, they were a familiar feature of the English countryside with some 26,000 throughout the country. Today, that number is decimated although there are still 25 in Somerset.
>
> From the middle ages to the late eighteenth century, their function was to provide the privileged with fresh pigeon meat during the winter months. This was either in the form of squabs – three-week-old birds – or mature pigeons. At this stage in our agricultural development, lack of feed at the time of year meant other livestock had been slaughtered and fresh meat was at a premium.
>
> This loft was part of the monastic estate of the Benedictine priory of Dunster, a cell of Bath Priory. It stands 8.5m high and has an internal di-

ameter of 4.5m. It would have produced something like two hundred squabs every week.

It is fascinating to peer inside and see the movable ladder. The circular wall has some five hundred openings in which the birds can nest. To reach these easily, the monks devised a simple vertical pole on a quite rudimentary bearing. Rudimentary or not, it has lasted for four centuries and is showing no signs of needing replacement.

High up, a crossbeam is attached to the vertical, and from this is suspended a ladder close to the wall. To reach any given nest, you simply pushed the ladder round to where it was needed. There was no struggling with an unwieldy ladder in a confined area. And they say that time and motion study is a twentieth century phenomenon.

The loft was taken over by the Luttrell family at Dunster Castle after the Dissolution and it is believed to have continued in use until around 1870. The building was extensively repaired in 1989. Work included re-pointing the exterior walls, a complete overhaul of the roof and structural timber-work, lime-washing the interior and re-laying the stone floor. The roof of the glover was finished with a new weathervane.

Continue along Priory Green, past the church to the road at the end and turn right, up the hill until you reach the Butter Cross.

This was once located in the High Street where the market was held. It was removed to this site in 1825, a thoughtful move. In those less enlightened days, it was not uncommon for something like this that had outlived its usefulness, to be broken up and the bits re-used in new construction work. As it is, much of the upper column is lost but the base and stump make a nice seating area.

Turn around at the Butter Cross and retrace your steps down the hill to a right turn some 70m along. Take the sharp right here, ignoring Hangers Way, up a track with a semi-concealed signpost indicating the way up Conduit Lane. This is a green lane. Follow the path up the hill, past St Leonard's Well.

For many years, the monks of Dunster obtained their water supply from this well. It was pumped from here to the priory.

The well-used path reaches the edge of some woodland. Here, another path leaves to the left, heading up to Grabbist Hill. Ignore it; although the walk is going there, it will take the scenic route.

The climb now eases. At the next fork, take the left-hand path which continues round the hillside before meeting a major junction of paths.

By now, you will have realised that this area of National Trust land is riddled with tracks and bridleways. Most are well signposted and, should you miss a turn, there will be another one soon.

At this junction, turn right, following the sign towards Alcombe. Keep straight ahead for some 900m, keeping to the left of the youth hostel. The track then takes a sharp left before meeting a road. Turn right here and a few metres along is a triangular junction. Turn left, over the stream and into Staunton Plantation.

By now, the walk is steadily uphill again as it passes through the ride. Keep straight along the main track as it bends and climbs until a left turn takes the walk out of the woodland and left at the next major junction where a fingerpost indicates the way back to Dunster.

Now, walking pretty much on the crest of this long ridge, the views open out before you. North is Minehead with the Welsh coast beyond. Barry is to the right and Llantwit Major left with Cardiff airport between. Down on the shoreline, look out for the steam railway operating. A trail of white smoke is laid as this tiny apparition snakes slowly on its way. You are actually within the Exmoor National Park but the best views of this area will come on other walks. For now, a taster can be seen in the west.

Walk along this ridge which develops into a wide track towards Grabbist Hill. Stay with this path past several partings of the way and, as the path eventually starts to fall away, turn right, downhill towards Dunster Castle, which is on the next piece of high ground.

The story goes that Mrs. Cecil Frances Alexander sat up here a century and a half ago and wrote the hymn *All Things Bright and Beautiful*. Born in Ireland in 1818, she married a bishop and published *Hymns for Little Children* in 1848. Also included in that collection was *Once in Royal David's City* and *There is a Green Hill Far Away*. These proved to be instantly popular and have remained so to this day. She was an accomplished writer of verse – both sacred and secular – and also composed ballads on Irish history. She died in 1895.

After 600m, pass through a gate and, keeping the cemetery on your right, walk past some allotments. On the right, another gateway gives access to a second cemetery. Walk through here along an avenue of trees to the road. Turn right and immediately left opposite the school into Priory Green (again). On the right is the lych-gate to the church.

St George's Church is well worth a stop. It is mainly a fifteenth century building with a flat roof over the south aisle that was built in 1450 and a fine wide waggon roof that dates from about 1500. Also built around the same time is the superb oak screen. This was ordered by an ecclesiastical court at Glastonbury so that the church could be partitioned, half for the monks, half for the villagers.

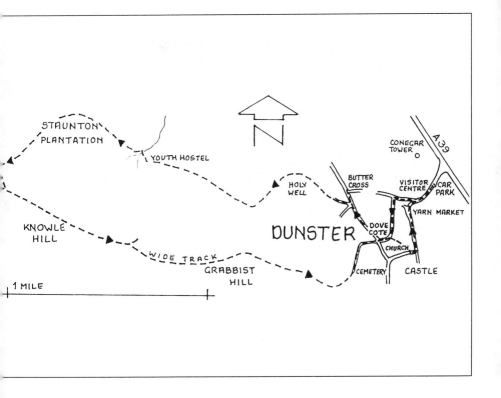

Behind the church was the site of the priory. And, should you be staying in Dunster, there is the chance of a really different treat. For just £6, you can arrange with the vicar to have the tower of the church floodlit for an evening. A chance to impress your wife/husband/lover/partner: what a delight. Also behind the church is a beautiful walled garden which was once part of the priory.

To reach this, return to the lych-gate and turn right. Opposite the dovecote is the entrance. Walk through there, down the slope diagonally right to a doorway in the far wall. Through here is another garden area along with an ancient tithe barn. This leads back out into High Street. Turn left and follow the road back to the car park.

There are, of course, several other attractions in this delightful area. Each merits a visit and only your time constraints will decide how much you see, or miss.

At the bottom of the High Street on the left is The Old Nunnery. This fourteenth century building is also strangely named: there were never nuns in Dunster. Slate-hung, this building actually acquired its name as recently(!) as 1769. Before that, it was known as the Chantry of St Lawrence and served as a guesthouse for visitors to the priory.

The principle attraction in the village is a little further along from here; Dunster Castle. A driveway leads to the entrance. It is of Norman origin, one of the many they built soon after the conquest in order to permanently subdue the locals. The original occupants were the de Mohuns.

Around 1375, it became home to the Luttrell family who have added and rebuilt down the years. It wasn't always this peaceful though. During the civil war, the Luttrells declared for parliament. Royalists seized the place and it was then besieged by Cromwell's lot for five and a half months during 1646. Evidence of this part of our turbulent history can be seen back at the yarn market. There is a mark on the roof where a cannonball, fired from the castle, landed.

There are some magnificent features inside the place. The carved staircase of 1681 is exquisitely beautiful, each panel made from a solid block of elm. An elegant plaster ceiling and painted leather panels add to the sheer splendour.

Looking north from the grounds of the castle is probably the best place to see Conygar Tower. Sadly, there is nothing dramatic or historic about this. It's just a good old English folly, built around 1770 and visible for miles around.

Then in 1976, it changed hands again. This time the National Trust took it over and now maintain it. The castle is open from April to September daily except Thursdays and Fridays, the grounds, all year.

But that's not the end of things, as you'll find if you walk either down Mill Lane or from the castle gardens. Dunster Water Mill dates from the seventeenth century and was restored to full order in 1979. But, according to Domesday, there was a mill on this site in 1086 so it has a fair pedigree. It is a real working mill and you can buy flour actually milled on site. It also has a tea room, and a good one too.

Although another National Trust site, it's operated and maintained by private funding so there's an admission charge to pay, even if you are an NT member. It's open every day from April to the end of September but closed on Saturdays in early and late season.

21. Tarr Steps

Distance:	2½ miles.
Start:	Tarr Farm, Liscombe, Dulverton, Somerset TA22 9PY. Tel: 851507.
Grid reference:	SS 868321
Parking:	Official car park 400m before the tea room. The only parking by the river is for disabled use.

Tarr Steps is a primitive clapper bridge, nicely in the middle of Exmoor with a quite deep ford to the right through the river Barle. Archaeologists have discovered Bronze Age tracks converging on this point which makes it quite an ancient crossing and actually considered to be the oldest and longest clapper bridge in the country.

The name 'Tarr' is unusual. It is probably derived from the Celtic "tochr" meaning a causeway. If this is so, it helps confirm its antiquity. That said, the earliest records of a bridge only date back to Tudor times. Horses and wheeled traffic can't use it of course, they have to be taken though the ford alongside.

Although constructed of huge lumps of Exmoor gritstone, the scene here is not quite as permanent as it looks. This river drains Exmoor and the force of flood water crashing down the valley has been known to wash away the top slabs, each weighing a ton or more. They don't get too far though and are replaced after the water level drops.

It is quite amazing to think that this apparently robust, squat structure could be uprooted by water, but it only goes to confirm the power of untamed water. For ease of working, every slab is now numbered so the gang who have the reconstruction work do not have a jigsaw facing them, as has happened in the past.

The last time they were uprooted was in August 1952. The torrential rain on Exmoor saw all but one slab washed away. That cloudburst was the one that created death and destruction at Lynmouth on the North Devon coast. Then, the East and West Lynn rivers became so full that they washed away trees. These became stuck at

Tarr Steps

bridges, creating a dam until pressure caused the bridge to fail, releasing a wall of water to the next barrier.

This continued to the sea at Lynmouth. Unfortunately, the confluence of these rivers had been altered to allow building work and that re-routing took no consideration of the possibility of that volume of water.

Over thirty people died that night and the damage was appalling. Even today, there are boulders at the bottom of the valley that were washed down in the torrent. To see the sheer bulk of these gives an impression of the power that struck a pretty little seaside village on that horrifying summer night.

Once, the gap between the Barle and the actual platform was much greater than it is today. Silting is the reason for this.

There is a delightful legend about Tarr Steps. The story goes that the devil built them so that he could sunbathe and vowed to destroy any creature attempting to use it as a bridge. A parson, sent to confront the forces of evil was attacked with the most foul and abusive language. But, our jolly preacher boy replied in a like fashion and the devil, so impressed by the holy man's vocabulary, conceded the crossing to the public.

As far as is known, the devil did not give away his sunbathing rights, a point to be observed if you are considering relaxing in the area.

Much of the Barle Valley is a Site of Special Scientific Interest. The woods contain a large proportion of ancient woodland where trees have grown since prehistoric times. There are sessile oaks to be seen, once used for tan bark and charcoal production. Eighty-five species of flowering plants, lots of lichens, butterflies and unusual birds also occupy this area.

Whenever you visit, it's gorgeous. Try January, when the river is full of winter hurry. Spring is beautiful; all is new and green. In summer, apart from the hordes of visitors, everything sparkles and the water makes a wet, whispering sound. Autumn: arguably the most compelling. The whole area is a cascade of colour and admirably fits George Ellis' description in his poem *The Twelve Months*. He saw autumn as 'Hoppy, Croppy, Droppy'.

The Tea Shop

The tea room at Tarr Steps is a venerable building, built in the sixteenth century and now owned and run by Richard Benn and Judy Carless. The range of food is vast and is good in the restaurant which serves cream teas, lunches and dinners.

The Walk

This is probably the simplest walk in this book; so far as directions are concerned. Leave the car park and turn left, down the hill. The tea room is on the right, at the bottom. Walk down to the river. Just before the crossing is a footpath sign pointing to the right. Follow this, alongside the Barle for almost a mile until you reach a foot-bridge over the water.

Cross over this and return down the other side of the water to Tarr Steps. Walk across the bridge and up the hill, back to the starting point.

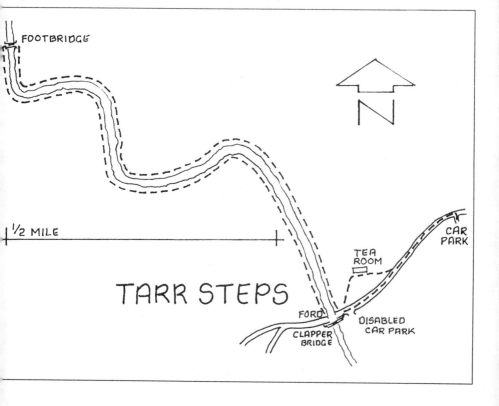

Although there are no ancient buildings, hills or dramatic ruins along this walk, it is a winner for the sheer delight of walking this corner of Exmoor. A word of warning though. After rain, the path can be extremely boggy and care should be taken. It is also a popular spot with visitors. An out of season midweek walk is almost guaranteed to produce a tranquil area utterly at odds with the situation that obtains of a high summer week-end.

One other interest hereabouts is that you can often meet long distance walkers. The steps are used by those people on the Two Moors Way. This links Dartmoor with Exmoor. It starts near Ivybridge which is on the south coast in the Plymouth direction, comes right up on to Dartmoor, down the other side, through the lush lowlands of Central Devon and up here to Exmoor. Finally, it goes over to Lynton where it joins the South West Coastal Path. After this short stroll, perhaps you are in the mood to challenge it. The Two Moors Way stretches a hundred and one miles if you fancy a crack at it.

22. Selworthy

Distance: 3 miles or 4 miles.

Start: Selworthy Church Car Park, Selworthy, north of the A39 Minehead to Porlock road.

Grid reference: SS 920468

Parking: As above.

Reaching this area of the county, Somerset has changed quite dramatically from the county we explored earlier. Gone are the flatlands with an occasional hill reaching steeply upwards. This is real hill country, the edge of Exmoor.

Selworthy

The Tea Shop

The selection is the **Periwinkle Cottage Tea-Room** – quality presentation, superb food and unmatched surroundings.

The Walk

Leave the car park, turn left and immediately left again, down the hill.

> Walking down the hill, there are toilets on the right, followed by an aged letterbox in the wall. This carries the legend 'VR', giving some indication of its antiquity.

Some 100m further down the hill, take a right turn and walk past Selworthy Farm and a footpath sign indicating the route to Allerford.

> This is unusual for this area in that it has a tiled roof and is of roughly rectangular shape. The chimney stack is also square; a direct contrast to the rounded ones that rule here.

After 100m, there is a fork in the lane; take the left-hand one which rapidly becomes a green lane as the road surface finishes. This rises gently and then falls to a left-hand bend some 600m along. At this point, a wide entrance with a gate will be discovered on the right.

Here also, it is time to make a decision on the one-mile extension. This takes in the village of Allerford. To omit this section, rejoin the walk description at *CONTINUATION*.

Bear left and continue along the narrow lane into the village of Allerford. This is reached across a steeply arched packhorse bridge with a ford to the left that can be almost impassable when the river Aller is full of winter hurry.

Across the bridge, turn right and, after 150m, The Museum of Rural Life is discovered on the right.

> Located in an old school, it was built during the 1830s when King William IV (aka Silly Billy) reigned. The exhibitions are arranged through three rooms. One is – fittingly – a Victorian schoolroom, another restored out as a house of a century ago. The kitchen, laundry and dairy are complemented by a huge Exmoor open hearth. The final room is a delight in that its contents change annually. This provides a continuing and on-going interest that encourages visitors to return again and again. There is also a garden and picnic area available. The place is open from Easter to October, Monday to Saturday and Sundays in high season.

After leaving the museum, re-trace your steps back to the bridge, turn left and walk up the lane to the right-hand bend where the wide gate is on the left.

CONTINUATION: Pass through the gate where there are three paths; take the right-hand one, straight up the hill. This is a bridle-way signposted to Selworthy Beacon and is a wide, quite well-used track through woodland.

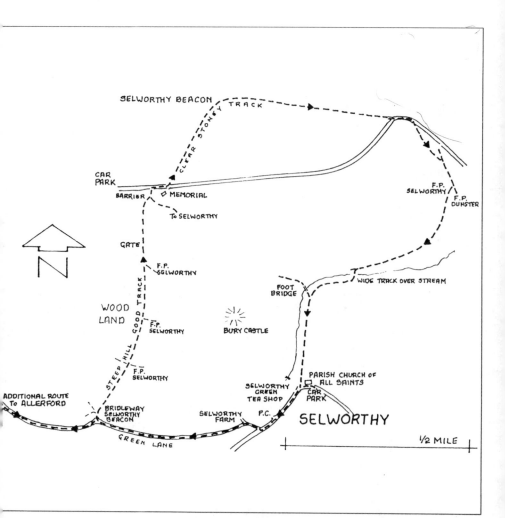

This is the steepest and longest climb encountered in this book and continues for nearly 900 breathless metres. During the climb, four separate paths will leave to the right, each marked Selworthy. They all offer an escape route for those even more unfit than the present writer; if such a soul exists!

The area also shows sign of extensive but thoughtful land management. That pestilential weed the rhododendron has taken over much of the undergrowth, smothering and killing what grew there before. Now, selective clearance has allowed these areas to recover and a carpet of wild flowers, heathers and mosses are re-establishing themselves, creating enchanting native woodland.

Passing through a gate, the path leaves the wooded area as the climb eases considerably and reaches a low wooden barrier.

Here is the final opportunity to cut short the walk as a track leads off to the right, signposted Selworthy.

Beyond this, a road. Turn right and after 50m, turn left.

At this point, on the right, a tiny solid stone shelter with four seats is located. This is a memorial to Sir Thomas Dyke Acland, a local landowner in remembrance of the time he devoted to both his children and grandchildren, teaching them to appreciate their environment. Sir Thomas was also responsible for Selworthy Green, as will be noted later.

This is a clear stony track, still uphill but considerably less steep that leads to Selworthy Beacon, some 308m (987ft) above sea level.

From here, you are on top of the world, which makes the hard climb well worth the effort. On a clear day you can see for ever: now that would make a nice line for a song.

Whichever way you look, there are views: south Wales, the Bristol Channel and other peaks both east and west. South though, is a different matter. Here, Dunkery Beacon, the highest point on Exmoor at 519m (1203ft).

Beyond the beacon, continue, following the same stony track down the other side, taking due note of a request by the National Trust (landowners hereabouts) not to stray off the path provided. This is to try and limit the serious erosion on this hillside.

This leads to a road; turn left and after 30m, take the path to the right which is signposted Selworthy and Dunster. After another 20m, this joins another path where the walk turns right and after yet another 20m, the Selworthy path – and this walk – turns right, steeply down into a combe.

On reaching the bottom, the walk turns left across a stream and then right. This takes the path alongside and to the left of the pretty stream.

Any children in your party will delight at this section. It is a typical Exmoor stream with endless possibilities for fun and games: and wet feet.

As the path sweeps left, a bridge over the stream brings the earlier escape route back to join the main path. Continue south, downhill.

After 400m, the path reaches a gate beside All Saints church. Beyond it, turn left for the car park or right through the gate into Selworthy Green.

Do not fail to explore this pretty little village. Apart from any other consideration, you will miss the tea room. Selworthy is built on a south-facing slope, looking across to Dunkery Beacon with the cottages built around a traditional village green. They are quite distinctive, cob-built and lime washed in pastel shades.

The village is part of the 5042ha (12,450 acres) Holnicote Estate, now owned by the National Trust. It was once owned by the Acland family, Sir Thomas being mentioned earlier. He was a benevolent nineteenth century gentleman who built the cottages in Selworthy Green as retirement homes for his workers.

There are fifteen farms and several other small villages or hamlets included in the estate and the NT has an office and shop in the village. This is not far from the Periwinkle Cottage Tea-Room which is first class. There are tables outside should you not want to experience the interior delights of this ancient building. The whole effect of quintessential England a generation ago is well created. It is open during the summer months only and offers a quite restricted menu of light meals, snacks and teas. But what it lacks in variety is more than made up for by quality.

The Parish Church of All Saints, Selworthy is small but fascinating. It looks quite plain on the outside; the early fifteenth century tower is Perpendicular in style although considerably earlier than the outer archway. Through an ancient heavy oak door, the interior is revealed.

The first thing that meets the eye is a huge iron-banded parish chest. Late sixteenth century, much of the wood is in an advanced state of decay and the whole thing is kept in place by a hugely incongruous shiny modern padlock and chain.

The pulpit is unusual in that the original sounding board above is still in place, as is the iron-framed hourglass that was used to time the sermon. Many a preacher today would benefit from such a device.

NB. If you enjoyed visiting All Saints Church, it is worth noting that, unusually for this corner of England, the church has two Chapels of Ease. These are small churches, subsidiary to the main and both are still in use. One is at Lynch. This is one mile beyond the Museum of Rural Life on the road to Bossington. It is early sixteenth century and the restored east window contains the seal of Athelney Abbey near Langport. This indicates that it was once owned by that Order which was established by King Alfred in 920.

The other, south of the main A39 in the direction of Minehead is St Leonard's at Tivington. This is thatched and has two open fireplaces. Again, the building date is somewhat obscure but is believed to be mid-fourteenth century. St Leonard's is another with monastic connections, this time with Montacute, the limited remains of which we saw during Walk 10. After the Reformation, it was put to a variety of uses and was not restored to worship until 1896. Both buildings are still in regular use.

NOTE: If the prospect of a severe climb does not appeal too much, it is possible to do this walk in the reverse direction. Then, the climb, although longer, is less steep.

23. Porlock

Distance:	4 miles.
Start:	Doverhay Car Park, Porlock, alongside the A39 trunk road.
Grid reference:	SS 887467
Parking:	See above.

Considering that Somerset has a long coastline, so far only Walk 13 which started at Burnham-on-Sea has taken much advantage of it. For this, the last walk in this book, we will enjoy a little more of a coastal walk.

Once again, it is a flat bit of Somerset, but look around: hills everywhere. To the right is Selworthy Beacon visited during Walk 22, and to the left, the notorious Porlock Hill which climbs at a twenty-five per cent grade (1 in 4).

Porlock weir

The Tea Shop

There is a surfeit of tea rooms available for this walk. Of several in Porlock, the selection is the **Camellia Tea and Coffee House** on the High Street.

The Walk

Leave the car park and walk down to the main road, past the 1930s style filling station and turn left. Cross the main road and take the first right, Sparkhayes Lane. Continue along this road until the paved section ends. Here, a slope to the right leads to a farm gate with a pedestrian gate to the left. A sign with arrow indicates 'Footpath – Do Not Walk In Lane'.

This lane is a narrow west country track with little room for vehicles let alone walkers. For your own safety, follow the sign.

Through the gate, a narrow walkway is formed at the edge of the field continuing alongside but above the actual road. After some 200m, this path ends, crosses a lane and picks up again at the other side, still heading north towards the sea, but separate from the dangerous lane.

On reaching the coast line, turn left and head west along the shore. The pebbles and boulders on the seaward side of the path delineate the walk clearly.

Looking due north, the south Wales coast is visible. As few maps show both sides of the Bristol Channel, looking at the Welsh pages, find Ogmore-by-Sea. This will give an indication of what you can see. To the left is Porthcawl which can fade into the mists whilst, on the right, the south Glamorgan coast strikes out south, towards Somerset and is usually clearly visible.

If anything is catching the sun over that side, it will be the white power station at Aberthaw which is on the outer edge of Cardiff.

On reaching a stile, cross and turn right along the road towards Porlock Weir.

The harbour at Porlock Weir is fifteenth century, the pubs sixteenth. The Anchor is the bigger one furthest along but they are actually a combined operation. There are also toilets in the car park by the shore. Amongst

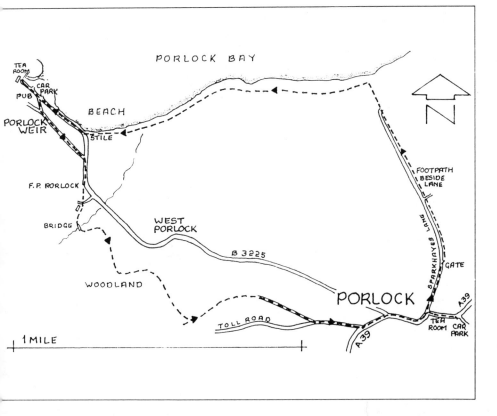

the many treasures you can discover here is another tea room called the Pieces of Eight. This one opens only during the season, offering a limited range of snacks and drinks.

It was in this tiny community where, a century ago, an epic lifeboat journey from Lynmouth ended, a journey – perforce – made overland. Lynmouth is a few miles west along the coast, but between the two places is Countisbury Hill, a mere 302 metres (991ft) high.

One stormy night a ship - the *Forrest Hall* – got herself into trouble in Porlock Bay. To effect a rescue, the lifeboat was needed. Lynmouth was the nearest but, with the wind from the north west, she could not be launched, so stormy was the sea. So what did they do? Oh, just whizzed the lifeboat along to Porlock Weir and launched it there. That bald statement conceals heroics above and beyond the call.

To get the boat over Countisbury Hill took a dozen or more horses and a hundred men. In the most appalling weather, they dragged that boat thirteen miles, taking eleven hours to do it. A wheel fell off the cart, so they used skids. But, they made it. And the result? In the intervening time, a tug had put to sea from Wales and taken the *Forrest Hall* in tow. If you should drive further west, you will appreciate the steepness of these hills and the sterling effort needed, ultimately to no avail.

Porlock itself was once by the sea. But it receded in the 11th century leaving Porlock Weir nearest the water. This then developed into a busy harbour, working up to a couple of hundred years ago before falling into relative disuse. Trade was mainly across the Bristol Channel. Coal and limestone came in, agricultural produce went out.

Porlock Weir is a delightful place to watch for birds. On the front you will get the usual selection of gulls and oystercatchers but a bit further inland, there are some good reed beds. Here, especially in the winter, you can see a wide variety of ducks which use this mild corner as a refuge. Teal, wigeon, shoveler and seemingly millions of the ubiquitous mallard. Yes, a good area.

There is also a literary connection, even tucked away down in this quiet corner. Robert Southey was not the best known English poet although he was a contemporary of Coleridge and Wordsworth. His fearful tale – *Bishop Hatto* – which tells how the wretched cleric received his comeuppance after cramming a large barn with the poor of his parish and then setting it alight, murdering the occupants. Southey actually stayed at the Ship and is supposed to have written some of his better-known verses in 1799, sitting by the pub's fire.

Start back along the road and, just beyond the Ship pub is a right-hand turn which passes **The Cottage** tea rooms. Continue uphill and at the top, bear left. When this lane reaches the main road, turn right and after 20m, as the road bears left, take the signposted footpath directly ahead signed Porlock.

After only a few metres, this path meets a road. Walk straight across, to the left of a long wooden building and uphill along the track. Cross a stream using the little footbridge and follow the path which circles gently left climbing up an easy slope on the far side of this pretty little valley.

This is a clearly waymarked route with blue symbols showing the way at regular intervals.

The path then drops away to the left, still waymarked, and signed West Porlock. Ignore the path that continues ahead which is unmarked.

At the next junction carry straight on towards Porlock, now ignoring the blue arrow which points the way to West Porlock. At the next junction, at the head of a very pretty garden, continue generally straight ahead, still heading towards Porlock which has now collected blue markers again. The path develops into a muddy lane and eventually reaches a road. Turn left, walk to the bottom, which is the A39, and turn left again. This becomes the High Street with lots of attractive shops. Cross over and call at the tea room, just before the car park.

The Camellia Tea and Coffee House is in the classic mould: a delightful building, steeped in tradition. Service is excellent and the offerings conform to the perception of what an English tea room should be about.

The cakes are home-made – the cherry and almond slices are particularly 'more-ish'. Beans on toast, crumpets and sandwiches are the main savouries and a bowl of good soup with a roll is extremely welcome in the winter months. The inevitable cream tea and a choice of tea blends go to make this into a delightful establishment. One large drawback though: the main A39 runs directly outside the door and traffic noise can be quite disturbing.

Tea Shop Walks – Spreading everywhere!

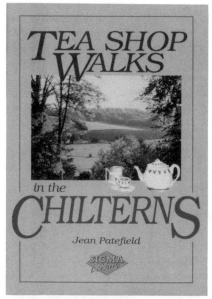

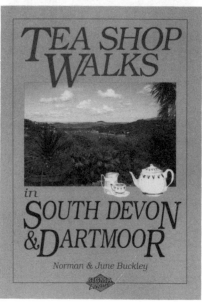

The Sigma Leisure Tea Shop Walks series already includes:

Cheshire

The Chilterns

The Cotswolds

Hampshire

The Lake District, Volume 1

The Lake District, Volume 2

Lancashire

Leicestershire & Rutland

North Devon

The Peak District

Shropshire

Snowdonia

South Devon

Staffordshire

Surrey & Sussex

Warwickshire

The Yorkshire Dales

Each book costs £6.95 and contains from 20 to 30 excellent walks: far better value than any other competitor!

CYCLING
in The West Country

by Helen Stephenson

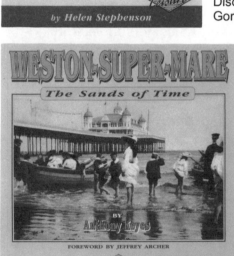

WESTON-SUPER-MARE
The Sands of Time

BY
Anthony Keyes

FOREWORD BY JEFFREY ARCHER

Also from Sigma Leisure:

Cycling in The West Country

This covers most of Somerset and much of Devon, built on Helen Stephenson's experience of running cycling holidays. Well-tested routes with plenty to see and visit. *£6.95*

Walks in Mysterious Somerset

Enjoy 27 walks in the company of walks and earth mysteries guru, Laurence Main. (Due early 1999). *£6.95*

Pub Walks in the Mendips

Discover the delights of the Cheddar Gorge and excellent hillwalking from such popular destinations as Weston-Super-Mare, Bristol and Wells. *£6.95*

Weston-Super-Mare: the sands of time

One of the few guides to Weston, this book by local author Anthony Keyes is packed with rare photographs, both old and new - "Little gem" WESTON & WORLE NEWS. *£6.95*

In case of difficulty, or for a free catalogue, please contact:
SIGMA LEISURE, 1 SOUTH OAK LANE, WILMSLOW, CHESHIRE SK9 6AR.
Phone: 01625-531035; **Fax:** 01625-536800.
E-mail: sigma.press@zetnet.co.uk **Web site:** www.sigmapress.co.uk
Please add £2 p&p to all orders. ACCESS and VISA welcome.